MW01096966

Last Summer On Lake Huron

Dave Dempsey

Copyright © 2017 Dave Dempsey

All rights reserved.

ISBN-13: 978-1976328374

DEDICATION

To Darlene & Derwin
the friends who reintroduced me to Lake Huron and whose unfaltering
generosity turned my life around

MAY

Natural forces always surprise us, be they large lakes or ancient methane.

May 20, 2017

The lake is inching up. Today's three waves of heavy rain will only drive it higher. A thunderstorm rocked the cottage around 4 a.m., another storm struck late in the morning, and a final downpour drenched the land and lake around 4 p.m. All told, an inch of rain must have fallen.

The beach route to the south, on which I last year enjoyed walking Fitz the Morkie (half-Yorkie, half-Maltese, basically a large looking Yorkie), is now closed off by the rising lake. Between the first two jetties, the lake intrudes all the way to the seawall. Last year there was a 15-foot-wide strip of sand.

The limits extend to the north, too. It is technically still feasible to trudge that way but the effort is greater than it was last year. Crashing waves have eroded the beach here and imported sand and stone elsewhere, undermining the general equity that prevailed in 2016. Passing from parcel to parcel now requires dragging one's self over a three- or four-foot-tall jetty or getting wet up to the shins. Fitz is not enthusiastic.

On gray mornings like this morning, mist encircles the square of beach at the foot of the neighborhood easement, giving it the feel of privacy.

Debbie the landlord and I chatted this morning when I brought her Sunday Starbuck's – purchased with a gift card she gave me. We discussed the water levels. She reminded me as she has done before that the lake has gone higher. During her first year of ownership in the mid-80s, a severe winter storm hurled ice boulders within a foot or two of her back windows. Like all who live on the shore, she has grown philosophical and tolerant of the lake's idiosyncrasies.

She said that the Army Corps convened a public meeting that winter and urged lakeshore property owners to move their houses at least 50 feet landward. She shook her head and laughed at the memory. It wasn't a particularly practical suggestion.

Debbie has become a good friend as well as the world's best landlord. In exchange for the coffee, I received a plateful of French toast and bacon. She's shared her spotting scope for over a year now so that brother Tom and I can discern the freighters' names.

I left Fitz here this evening to go to the gym. When I returned the final storm had ceased and the sun had burst loose from the clouds. As usual I bent over to pet Fitz, who had awoken from a nap, when my glance turned to the window. A stripe of the lake is always visible between two houses to the north of Debbie's and in that corridor, a freighter was profiled in brilliant light. Small as if a toy, the reddish freighter crept quietly southward as I watched. It was a scene of subtlety that I will not see when I move.

Tonight, the lake is not thudding against the shore. That's the exception, not the rule. Sometimes I swear the ground under this cottage shakes when the waves are particularly strong. I am 250 feet inland.

May 22, 2017

The lake passed through several moods today, but so did the sky. Clouds mostly concealed the sun until early afternoon, when the lake changed from gray to summer blue. This evening it mirrored the purple of the heavens. Quite by accident, I took one of my best smart phone photos of the lake then. The water has the sheen of mercury.

While Fitz and I scratched in the sand, a couple approached from the north with a teacup Yorkie on a leash. Arriving at the stream – actually a county drain that empties into the lake – they halted and turned around. Rather than lifting the dog over the jetty under its belly, the man lifted it by the leash, dangling it like a fish on a line. It sounds more inhumane than it looked. The dog squeaked a little but quickly recovered once the man deposited it on the sand.

A dead bird rested in the bed of rocks at the base of the little bluff overlooking the water all day. Fitz took a look at it each time, and I forgot to keep him clear of it each time. He tends to try eating such things. This time he sniffed and pawed but took no nourishment.

As often happens, a vessel has anchored several miles offshore for two days. Marinetraffic.com pronounces it the *Harbor Fountain*, an oil and chemical tanker. The website is precise enough: the ship has a gross tonnage of 11,880, a length and breadth of 144.06 meters by 23 meters, and was built in 2011. It left Port Weller, Ontario on May 17th at 16:40.

I have asked knowledgeable people several times why ships habitually anchor in far southern Lake Huron and have received varying answers. Some, it appears, are awaiting a licensed Great Lakes pilot to guide them through the narrow Port Huron/Sarnia-to-Lake Erie corridor. Others, like this one, may be awaiting cargo – perhaps the refining of product in Sarnia? Another cause is the need to ride out a fierce gale in safety. Only once since I've lived here have I seen this: seven vessels anchored within view for over 36 hours.

I've written elsewhere about the fascination freighters inspire in me and apparently in others. It's simplest to say that their loneliness out on the great waters gives them an appealing vulnerability, and their origins and destination in faraway places imbues them with romance. But why romance also attends the shipwrecks, I don't know. A kind of cult has formed around them. Although the cult members don't risk their lives like storm chasers, there's the same adolescent thrill in nature's destructive powers.

For one of the few times this spring, I have opened the window to the night air. Amazingly, for the second straight evening, the lake is nearly still.

May 23, 2017

At 8:25 p.m. the *Harbor Fountain* still languishes offshore.

I took Fitz twice today to Fort Gratiot County Park on the lake for 15-minute walks. A friend directed me to it in February 2015 when Fitz and I enjoyed a winter retreat here. In the deep snow and harsh cold of that winter, we enjoyed the park almost in solitude.

The park bustles for a little more than three months of the year, beginning this weekend. Large groups occupy the gazebos, families snatch up all the picnic tables, teens play Frisbee in the sand while kids rule a small playground, and the smell of cooking meat is inescapable. I try to avoid the park on those days. Too many people for Fitz.

What distinguishes the park is a memorial. It commemorates not a politician or general but 22 men who died for water, Lake Huron water specifically. While honoring the dead, it expresses ambivalence inherent in the fulfillment of an institutional dream that has unintended consequences.

The project that took the lives of the 22 men on December 11, 1971 had been a dream of the Detroit water department since the late 1800s. The water supplied by the utility's intake in the Detroit River was adequate to meet the city's needs, but even then, there was thought of population growth to the north. That would require a new source of water. By virtue

4

of both proximity and quality, Lake Huron was the choice for the new water source. A point five miles offshore from what is now the county park was chosen for the intake.

The memorial consists of three features: a plaza of bricks etched with the names of the loved ones who perished in the disaster and other individuals and groups who purchased and contributed them; the statue of a symbolic project worker, and a state historical marker. The last is especially noteworthy. It is literally two-faced. The two sides of the marker could not be more different in tone.

One side stresses the tragic human losses and the terrible power of the explosion: "…[A] shotgun-like blast claimed the lives of twenty-two men working on a water intake tunnel beneath the bed of Lake Huron. A pocket of methane trapped within a layer of ancient Antrim shale fueled the explosion. An exhaustive inquiry determined that drilling for a vertical ventilation shaft from the lake's surface had released the trapped gas…The blast created a shock wave with a speed of 4,000 miles an hour and a force of 15,000 pounds per square inch. Witnesses reported seeing debris fly 200 feet in the air from the tunnel's entrance."

The other side emphasizes the project itself as a triumph of man: "In 1968, to serve the water needs of a growing population, the Detroit Metro Water Department began work on the Lake Huron Water Supply Project. This massive feat involved erecting a submerged intake crib connected to a six-mile intake tunnel beneath Lake Huron. The mechanical mole that dug the 16-foot wide tunnel bored through the bedrock beneath the lake at a rate of 150 feet a day. The project excavated more than one billion pounds of rock. The water treatment plant pumped clean water into an 82-mile system of water mains supplying Detroit and Flint. When finished in 1973, the $123 million system boasted a capacity of 400 million gallons a day."

One has to wonder whether this mentality was partially culpable. Pride in a monumental public works project may have promoted hubris, or contributed to denial by the managers if someone pointed out the danger. Carelessness or ignorance may also have been to blame.

Natural forces always surprise us, be they large lakes or ancient methane.

May 24, 2017

When I took the train and automobile back from Chicago on May 12, I went from one lobe of a Great Lake to the other. Lake Michigan-Huron is one water body, despite its appearance to the eye and mind. But when I recognize the unity of the lake, I feel connected to friends almost 250 miles away. We're in the same watershed and tread a single uninterrupted shore.

When North Americans are asked to identify the largest lake in the world, many of them single out Lake Superior. But they're wrong. Russia's Lake Baikal is the largest by volume. Lake Michigan-Huron is the largest by surface area at 45,300 square miles. Superior is a mere 31,700 square miles and Baikal, a merely mere 12,248.

Why isn't Lake Michigan-Huron widely recognized by the public? It has a single water level. But nature has designed it in such a way as to fool the human mind. Linked only by a five-mile strait, the Michigan lobe and the Huron lobe resemble fraternal twins. One is dotted by large cities, and heavily industrialized at one end. The watershed of the other is lightly populated and the lake/lobe has been all but forgotten. Huron gets no respect.

The converse of the above is the remarkable diversity of Lake Michigan-Huron. Sandy and stony shores, majestic cities and legally designated wilderness, sturgeon and salmon, the feeling of the north and the anxious intensity of the Midwest, the maple leaf and the red, white and blue. There is no other lake close to it in all the world.

So, here's to Lake Michigan-Huron.

May 25, 2017

The *Harbor Fountain* was gone this morning. I have a little twinge of loss whenever one of these guests suddenly leaves. Their presence is steadying and comforting.

Tom is here. At the moment (11:35 p.m.), he is standing out back by the water in drizzle and darkness while I anchor a comfortable couch in dry air. He sees the setting here with fresh eyes. Mine occasionally grow weary and their news is received with no sensitivity. Ostensibly, Tom is waiting as two freighters pass from north to south, but even their gleaming beauty is only part of a much larger whole.

I will not romanticize that whole. In the dark, dampness and unseasonable cold, it is forbidding out there. It is not necessarily friendly or benign. But it offers a welcome shift for the senses, shocking the system out of complacency. I have been too complacent to join him.

May 26, 2017

I strolled down to the beach around 8:30 in the evening to find my friend's cousin, his son, daughter-in-law and two young grandchildren. The cousin's granddaughter, probably about three years old, entered the frigid water several times, screamed with delight and lingered a minute. I had forgotten how a child, while vulnerable, can sometimes withstand what an adult finds miserable. I played in the snow for hours as a child and now wouldn't willingly spend more than a few seconds doing so.

This little girl was delighted with the fresh air and the big lake. I enjoyed watching her jubilation. She shared it by smiling at all of us in turn.

The sky under which we stood reminded me of heaven. By that I mean it began with the specific and transitioned to the general with height and distance. At the very top the clouds diffused into a nebulous pool. The brightest white and deepest purple reflected off the still waters.

Debbie met Fitz and me as we returned from the beach tonight. I explained who the visitors were. She quickly approached them and encouraged them to use her beach which, although small, is measurably larger than the communal one. She has opened her house to me, brought me dinner and breakfast and monitored my health. She is generous by nature. I have yet to collect all of her lake stories.

Tom's visit ended quietly this morning, as the clouds persisted. I was sorry about the foul weather that dogged his time here. I derive a great deal of pleasure from *his* pleasure in the lake. He will be especially happy on the first warm day he visits, when he can claim his spot on the far south end of the beach at Lakeport State Park.

He took me there once last summer. I understood his enjoyment of the place. While the beach to the north was clotted with crowds and rang with the cries of children, calm prevailed where he prefers to sun himself and enter the lake. Most important, the lake rather than people commanded the scene. That day, the water was softly turning under a brilliant August sun. The lake was intimate with us.

I never trod the beach this winter, but I did wander through the closed park and took away glimpses of the lake. Although on some days in the dark of the year the lake can be fetching, it is typically hostile to any notions of a calm relationship with humans. I never touched the water.

Of course, the park was a somber place even on winter days of maximum light. I passed the bathhouse and other places where Tom and I had been the previous August. In January, each is accompanied by a poignant memory.

May 27, 2017

I woke up at 5:45 this morning, early enough to see the sunrise, but the delicious paralysis of my limbs in a warm bed intervened. I regret not getting up, but I do have photos of at least 25 different sunrises over the lake. And I mean different. Each is distinct from the rest.

One of the joys of meeting the lake at sunrise is the typical quiet of the water. Having often thrashed the afternoon and evening before, the lake seems to have rested overnight. This calms me. And as always, the freshness of a new day fosters hope.

I haven't seen much of the lake today, except long-range glimpses through the cottage window. Debbie has company that includes a sweet black Lab, but the presence of another dog on the property sends Fitz into a frenzy. Hence, we spent the bulk of the day indoors. On such days, the lake is a gleaming bauble but not much else.

On the landward side of the property, Memorial Day weekend is evinced by a flock of automobiles. An extra six or eight line the communal driveway. Although families and friends observe holidays anywhere, the lake is a special draw. It's like camping beside a mountain. The lake is the dominant feature and is with you all day and night.

After writing the above, on impulse I drove Fitz to Lakeside Park, hoping fresh turf would please him. At 8 p.m. the park had emptied out, except for one family, a few stragglers and a volleyball game among shirtless young men. The lake loomed like a whale but almost no one gave it a glance.

8

While Fitz urinated on each trash bin, I observed the lake and sky. Pink decorated the far eastern rim, with a shelf of fog below it. For the first time this season the small boats of sport anglers dotted the lake surface. Out of sight to the south a freighter sounded its horn obnoxiously, finally coming into view as the *St. Laurent*, on its way to Thunder Bay.

As always, I noted the sign at the southern terminus of the park beach, where private property begins. It allows that anyone may walk the beach even past the park boundary as long as he or she doesn't go beyond the ordinary high-water mark. Property owners don't like it, but the common law public trust doctrine grants the right; no one can privatize the land beneath the Lakes – whether that land is perpetually or only occasionally underwater. Interestingly, or perversely, Ohio courts say the right only extends to what is submerged; so there you have to keep one foot in the water.

I'm not sanguine that this right of passage will endure. The lushly-endowed private property rights lobby could help buy enough seats on the Michigan Supreme Court to narrow, if not eliminate the application of the doctrine, whose survival after 1500 years (reaching back to the Romans) should be foolproof.

May 29, 2017

The *Harbour Fountain* is back, anchored again several miles offshore. The lake remains quiet, thanks to an uncharacteristic break in the wind.

While waiting for the visiting dog to vacate and open the way to a bark-free beach visit, I checked the latest on Great Lakes levels. Each of the five lakes is well above its long-term average, but Ontario is in crisis.

My lake, Michigan-Huron, has risen 5 inches over the 30 days preceding May 19. Michigan-Huron is forecast to rise 2 inches before June 19. Lake Ontario has risen 18 inches to a level 31 inches higher than a year ago. That is unfortunate not just for lakefront property owners, but for a lake level plan concluded only in January by my former employer, the International Joint Commission.

After a staggering 16 years of study, the Commission in December ordered implementation of the plan. The primary change from prior lake level plans affecting Lake Ontario was its goal of improving ecosystem health and

9

diversity on Lake Ontario and the upper St. Lawrence River. Mimicking natural lake level changes, the plan was designed to restore 64,000 acres of coastal wetlands with associated benefits for fish and wildlife. The primary mechanism of the plan is regulation of the outflow from the Lake at the Moses-Saunders Dam.

This was a breakthrough. When the Commission approved the initial plan in the late 1950s, protecting the ecosystem was not considered. It's not likely anyone involved used the word "ecosystem." The new plan is an attempt to live in harmony with the ecosystem, not just to produce more fish and wildlife, but on the assumption that humans will benefit, if immeasurably and in the long run, from doing so.

But New York state property owners argued that the new plan would allow levels to increase enough to flood their lakefront holdings. And, just a few months later, record rains have in fact resulted in flooding. It's a coincidence – the Commission has permitted dramatically increased flow out of the lake to alleviate conditions – but try telling that to an aggrieved property owner who's convinced "the government" has chosen muskrats over people.

The Commission's fact sheet says, "Water levels on Lake Ontario and the St. Lawrence River are primarily determined by rain, snow, wind and other natural factors." It's true. Humans are not yet able to play God with the Great Lakes. But as long as I've followed these matters, some people have attributed every significant rise and fall of the lakes to a conspiracy coordinated by the Commission. Without the Commission's help, the Lakes fluctuate naturally six to seven feet.

Finally, toward sunset, Fitz and I made it down to the lake. I would like to project my emotional set onto Huron and call it frustrated. It slapped at the beach in annoyance, hungry for the drenching storm that fell apart just before reaching this area. I thought I had had enough rain but the prospect of a weather drama, a good spring thunderstorm, appealed to me. Thunder sounded in the distance but only a light spittle fell.

Fog continues to hover just above the water surface maybe a mile out. That's because the air temperature was 72 and the water temperature around 48, according to the Sea Grant Coast Watch. I'm wondering when the lake will become swimmable. It's always a short season at this latitude.

The lights of the anchored *Harbor Fountain* are visible offshore. I'm almost fond of that vessel.

May 30, 2017

I spotted the first water skier of the year out on the lake this morning. She was wearing a wetsuit. Good thing, because her motorboat pilot was in a hurrying mood, making a sharp turn that I thought might topple her. But she didn't fall when within my eyesight.

A little later I returned to the shore to enjoy a flotilla – a paddleboat, sailboats and power boats. The last make a drone that is both grating and cheering. It's a sound of summer. Summer is welcome here along the shore even if ushered in by churning engines.

The afternoon lent itself to lake picture-taking as clouds eclipsed sun and towering cumulonimbus shot up, reflecting vivid white off the lake surface. The other day I saw clouds that went from specific to general with height. Today it was the reverse. A finely etched anvil sat atop a cloud dropping an opaque film of rain.

As evening came, the sky cleared, helping me breathe again. The last day of a holiday weekend floods me with anxiety as I contemplate a return to work. This has been going on for 40 years. It doesn't matter whether I'm comfortable in my job. Body memory rules.

I'm so accustomed to having the beach to myself that it only dawned on me today that I'd best keep Fitz off between now and my moveout date in August. He's in the habit, which I haven't discouraged, of pissing in the sand each morning. And afternoon. That's fine in December, but not in June, July and August.

While down there today I noticed the outlet of the county drain had moved again. It snakes back and forth with each storm, from north to south. For a couple of dry weeks last summer, the drain never reached the lake. Fitz tries to drink from it but I restrain him whenever I notice. Debbie says the drain receives farm waste, and farm waste can mean animal waste, and that can mean e. coli. Upstream of the outlet he can drink all he wants.

I'll be getting up at 5:30 a.m. and be (I hope) on the road by 6 a.m. I plan to pay 60 seconds of my respects to the lake before I go. I'm wistful every time I must say goodbye to the lake to attend to business inland. I frequently wonder why anyone in a shoreline area chooses to live more than a quarter mile from the lake. Living inland around here is like favoring broccoli over mac and cheese.

May 30, 2017

As expected, this morning's journey was disorienting. At 5:58 I stood on the shore of Lake Huron as its waters made relaxed sounds and the sun lifted itself up from the horizon. At about 11:30 I walked into my new office in Traverse City 245 miles away. Yes, that office is only 2 blocks from a bay of the same lake I left, Huron-Michigan. But it feels like a separate galaxy.

Like many humans, I don't appreciate what I have until I lose it or leave it, and this morning I'd have been overjoyed to stay and watch the first hour of the day over the lake. The new day had the tang of summer. Here it feels like late March.

Sunrises will remain in memory as the signal experience of my two years on Lake Huron. I have seen dozens, few of them comparable. I've learned to appreciate that a lake sunrise, or sunset, is far more beautiful with scattered clouds. I should have figured that out long ago.

The clouds don't just provide contrast, but lend an interest of their own. In the winter dawn, I have sometimes seen long trains of lake effect snow clouds racing from northwest to southeast, their tendrils of precipitation dragging on the lake surface.

May 31, 2017

If there is a redeeming feature of social media, it is that you can spread beauty to many people almost effortlessly. Meeting a friend today in Grand Rapids, I was pleased that he remarked on my Facebook album of Huron sunrises. He seemed, however, nonplused that I have fallen in love with Huron. It is far more common for residents of the Great Lakes State to embrace Lake Michigan and its evenings.

I'm starting to think of the Huron crowd as a scrappy band of no social prominence who fight for their lake. Lake Michigan real estate is coveted by the Chicago and Oakland County elite. The sunsets and the dunes are part of the attraction, but the biggest attraction may be the competition to make a prime buy.

I've begun looking back at the Huron years, both of them, and to appreciate the healing they provided. I'm attached enough to the lake that I'm once again weighing whether I can keep both places. It will take a lottery win, but at least I now have a compelling rationale for buying lottery tickets.

JUNE

I think tonight of a career spent working on the abstraction of the Great Lakes and now two years spent living against the reality of a Great Lake.

June 1, 2017

The Great Lakes are always with us in Michigan, if we just pay attention. It begins with the news: the President today announced he's pulling us out of the Paris climate agreement. The harm this decision will cause sweeps across the economy and the environment generally, but it emphatically damages the Great Lakes. Climate change is making weather more unpredictable in our watershed – record floods, record low ice cover, wild temperature swings. It's changing the array of species that inhabit the land and water here. Trump's folly hurts the Great Lakes.

June 2, 2017

After giving a speech near Roscommon tonight I drove only 45 minutes toward home. In younger days, I'd have forged on and gotten home at 1 a.m. It's too dangerous now. My night vision is terrible. But I'm thinking how nice it would be to stand by the lake in the dark and listen to the contented lapping of the water on sand. Tomorrow night.

June 3, 2017

Depleted, I have spent most of the day since I returned lying on the couch or bed. But Fitz and I have made it down to the water twice. Tonight was the most striking. As we approached the beach the lake horizon looked lopsided. It was fog. Tendrils of it waved from the rim of the sky.

The environment was bleached, all dull grays and whites. But the patient rhythm of the small waves was pre-eminent.

June 4, 2017

It's not the lake's fault I'm becalmed. The constant back and forth to Traverse City means I need a day to adjust before I feel fresh enough to observe and record.

Why Traverse City? Because it's the birthplace and home of FLOW (For Love of Water), where I began working in April. There is no other place I'd rather work. The founder, Jim Olson, is a hero of mine. An attorney, he has had nature for a client for decades. The director, Liz Kirkwood, is an effervescent, indefatigable administrator and friend. I believe passionately in their cause, protection of the public trust. But I began the job without having a place to live in Traverse City. So it's motels or friends during the week up north, Lake Huron on weekends.

My friend and his family are down the street at their cottage. I happened to meet his dog and him while giving Fitz an 8 a.m. bathroom break beside the beach. I mentioned the high water but from where we were standing it wasn't evident. Only on the far side of the next jetty is the tearing away of the sand evident. Such is the apparent capriciousness of jetties. They may enhance one's property while damage occurs to one of the next couple living down current.

One of my political memories involves a state senator from Muskegon who fought the DNR to get approval of some kind of innovative groin that was going to save lakeshore property owners. The DNR regarded it as witchcraft and refused to issue a permit until the senator tied its approval to any hope of his support for an adequate agency budget. He was on the appropriations committee and had much influence over state spending. So DNR issued the permit, the jetty was installed and I never heard another word. I guess it wasn't a miracle cure. Surprise.

"I'm governor of a saturated sponge." That's what the boss, Governor Blanchard, told a reporter in 1986 after a tour of a portion of the Lake Michigan shoreline where houses were falling into the lake during a period of even higher lake levels. By 1988 the upper Lakes had fallen below the average. This time levels could go either way. Climate change has altered everything.

June 5, 2017

After a possible sunrise viewing tomorrow, I will be away from this place and this lake for 10 days. It's not a happy prospect.

Fitz and I wandered inside just now after a windblown visit to the shore. The cold northeast wind holds strong after 24 hours, chopping open the water like a multitude of knives to reveal white viscera. And yet – its presence, in storm or sun, offers comfort. I will have to carry the feeling with me to Traverse City and Minnesota and back.

I think tonight of a career spent working on the abstraction of the Great

16

Lakes and now two years spent living against the reality of a Great Lake. The abstraction comes arm in arm with adjectives like majestic and nouns like bounty, public testimonials, and political betrayal. The reality is a test, almost equal measures of beauty and bleakness. The bleakness is simply the banality of the everyday, the loss of wonder that can come from familiarity.

In intimate relationships, it is sometimes difficult to surmount that banality and recover the wonder. With the lake it is a little easier. Its raw beauty and power strip away the complacency and reawaken the senses. And of course, it has no emotional demands to make. It just is. It does not inspire my resentment. So the wonder returns.

Those who would protect the Great Lakes should live by them a while. They will find a refreshing, if intermittent wellspring of hope and faith.

June 6, 2017

I'm again in Traverse City, but the day began by my lake. I had set the alarm for 5:40 so as to be able to catch the sunrise, but clouds obscured it. At around 6:30 I did walk outside with Fitz to capture a few images of a moody sky reflecting off subsiding waters. The look of October characterized the scene, and the air was autumn fresh. To the north, a freighter's silhouette cruised along the horizon.

The lowest clouds drifted from the northeast like tufts of gray dryer lint. The higher clouds were waffle weave, letting some light through.

This is a scene I've come to love: a new day over a new lake. The lake and sky constantly renew themselves. I find hope and solace in it.

It's become commonplace to refer to the Great Lakes as treasures. But do people who possess literal treasure take it for granted as we often do the Great Lakes? I suspect most count it, feel bolstered by it, are sure they can rely on it in hard times. And want to add to it.

One source of my appreciation of the Great Lakes was the childhood trips to visit Grandma and Grandpa in the Upper Peninsula. And I do remember being impressed, even awed by the blue horizon. The truth is more complicated. When it comes to childhood, it's difficult to discern the beginning of anything. It's a mist. I remember being in the backseat of the family car with a big lake on the right. I've guessed that this was on M-28 heading west toward Marquette but who knows?

And was that the primal source of wonder, or was the 1981 backpacking trip to Pictured Rocks the foundation of my commitment even though by then I was 24? I do vividly remember that Sunday afternoon before the Monday morning awakening. I remember the stunning clarity of the deep water as we looked down from the cliffs. And I remember the thunder that rolled out across the mammoth lake, a deep, slow growl. I was beginning to fall in love.

Love isn't enough. It never is. Acts are necessary. I can't fault the rest of the Great Lakes population for not doing enough because I don't do enough. I haven't improved my consumption habits. I still buy products whose manufacture or disposal harms the ecosystem with microfibers or synthetic chemicals.

And so the health of the lakes stagnates or even falters.

June 7, 2017

In 1986, I put together a policy initiative for the Governor called "Great Lakes 2000." (It was annoyingly renamed Great Lakes 2001 by our otherwise first-class press secretary, who belonged to the camp that says new centuries begin in years that end with 01.) One of its features was the goal of cleaning up Michigan's 14 contaminated areas of concern (mostly rivers, bays and harbors with toxic sediments) by 2000. I believe 2 have been delisted and others, if they ever are, may not be delisted until after 2030. The original goal was proposed in good faith. We didn't know how difficult it would be to clean these messes up. The sins of the fathers.

It's interesting to me that while shaking my head at the hubris of previous generations who treated the Great Lakes like a waste receptacle, I and others had the hubris to believe we could manipulate the lakes back to health in relatively little time. The sins of the sons and daughters.

I'm sitting in a motel room in Traverse City reviewing the last two years of life on Lake Huron, trying to select the top two or three memories. High on the list is the first photo I took of the lake from the cottage. It's as lovely as a painting. No people are in it. Debbie's pine stands with its arms out, reaching like Gatsby for the green light, except the green light is snuffed out until dusk. The sky is a calming blue, the lake an oceanic gray green. It's an idealized scene made real. It should have brought me calm and joy. Yet I could barely function. I had no plan. I had just ended up here in an alien

18

land.

One of the comforts of the photo was that it reminded of scene from a favorite book of my childhood, *Mystery in the Pirate Oak* by Helen Orton. The mystery in itself stirred my imagination, but I'm thinking now about the closing scene, after its resolution. Grandmother Hale, Chad and Ellie go to the beach to celebrate. It's difficult to convey the poignancy a child feels about an imaginary outing of a patched-together family looking out over big waters, where love is openly expressed, but that ocean scene was so powerful that its attendant emotions warm me 52 or 53 years later.

June 9, 2017

I drove to Frankfort to visit Joan Wolfe last evening. Aside from seeing a dear friend (and architect of Michigan's Environmental Protection Act), the most memorable moment of the trip was suddenly beholding flickering silver Lake Michigan from the moraine high above the city. It is one of the most impressive highway views in Michigan. It's one that builds pride, unreasonable pride since I had nothing to do with its creation. I want everyone to see this stunning vision of hope.

June 10, 2017

Tom and I teamed on a 630-mile drive from Traverse City to our cousin's house in Minnesota yesterday. It cost us a punishing 14 hours ending at 1 a.m. One interlude, which salvaged the day, was a stop at the boardwalk and beach at Manistique. Out over the lake was a summery pale yellow haze, through which a warming sun drilled. The water had a slight tint of green near the shore, possibly a warning signal of a rough algae season ahead. Still, the water was inviting to two parched travelers – though we could not drink it, the lake would replenish our spirits.

Amazingly, down by the breakwater swimmers splashed in the shallows.

June 14, 2017

If you can be homesick, can you be Huron-sick? Not sick of Huron, but sick for it. Missing it. Not feeling it. Anxious to be near it again.

After 10 days, if all goes well I will see her again tomorrow night. I'm pleased. Tom and I drove all along the northern and northwestern rim of Lake Michigan going to and returning from Minnesota, but it was scenery, not personal. I saw the beauty but it didn't penetrate my armor.

It's poignant that I may soon be saying goodbye to Huron. I need to observe, listen, and feel on these remaining days with her. Including tomorrow.

June 16, 2017

I arrived back here on the big lake late last night and did not go down to the water. Debbie's house had still-alert occupants, foiling my plans. This morning Fitz and I explored the beach briefly. The waters were busy in a moderate wind. A transparent plastic spoon was the only human flotsam. I look forward to three days of observation.

Late morning – back to the shore. The lake has risen further. The formerly sandy, open path to the south is drowned in several inches of water that run up to the seawall. Looking over it to the south, I could see only a narrow strip where an inviting, spacious beach thrived last year.

Although a friend wanted to link the epic rains and record level of Lake Ontario this spring to climate change in a report with which I'm assisting, I don't think it's wise. You just can't tie one season's weather to climate.

The other observation just now was a cruising leisure craft a mile or so offshore, broadcasting that familiar sound, a deep bass cough, that signifies summer.

Evening – I had two more encounters with the lake. Fitz and I strolled under a hot sun at Fort Gratiot park. Families were out, occupying prime beach real estate. Two little girls asked to pet Fitz, who was more guarded with them than he is with adults. But the lake, the silvery heaving lake, was the organizing principle. Few would enter the park if it didn't exist.

Late this afternoon, I joined Debbie's family on the cement shelf, overlooking the lake, that others call a patio. We sat under a gray sky. For one of the few times this year, the waters were busy -- with kayakers and canoeists. The brief season is on.

This evening the sun came out just long enough to strike a red-hulled vessel edging north. The *Federal Baltic* is on its way to Burns Harbor, Indiana. This 34,500-ton freighter was as silent as a stealthy burglar.

June 17, 2017

Why do sweeping vistas move me so? Others may enjoy the view from a mountaintop, but I see as much or greater beauty from an elevation of six-foot-one above the lake. A seemingly infinite sky and lake stir me. Together, they transform my imagination to possibility and the mystery of eternity. The unknowables. There is something comfortable, too, in a tangible demonstration of human scale. In weight, we are individually to Lake Huron like a half dozen trophy salmon. That pleases me.

We were sitting around the office in Traverse City this week talking about one of our major programs, the battle against water privatization. One of the group said we should tell a prospective funder that with financial support we can "turn the tide." That immediately led to a discussion of whether the Great Lakes have tides. They do, but less than two inches. They also have tsunamis, but a foot or two only. In so many numeric ways they can't rival the oceans. But at the same time, they offer an intimacy that no ocean can.

June 18, 2017

I will never again live in a dwelling where I can sit at my desk and detect the mood of one of the largest lakes in the world.

Tonight's mood at the lake was of summer vacation. The clouds hurried out of town, dry and cool air took command, and the lake laughed softly. I could have stood there all night treasuring the fragrance of the season and the deep blue water.

June 19, 2017

A pleasant, mild morning yielded to a cool, damp afternoon. Thunder has been rolling through the neighborhood. The lake remains tranquil.

Debbie's son, who left for California after our conversation, confirmed that during low water times at least 100 feet of additional lakebed was exposed immediately off her property. As Debbie said, you could walk a mile south or more between mainland and lake without getting your feet wet.

The Lakes are cyclical. We need to accept that. They don't conform to our wishes. They are not wholly wild after four centuries of European use and much tampering, but they retain an element of the wild.

Today's notable vessel was a jet ski, officially termed "personal watercraft." One bearing a middle-aged man raced past as I stood on the beach. He went from my far left to my far right in 20 seconds. The gunning engine and slap of water against the PWC could be said to taint the lake experience. In fact, when PWCs became popular I loathed them and the people attached to them. But in old age I am trying to relax my judgments. Their pilots may be wasting time and fuel, but at least they are outside. And from that, incidentally, may come acts of stewardship.

June 20, 2017

In the hour before sunrise, the light over the lake is a secret whispered only to a few. At 5:38 this morning, before returning to Traverse City, I lingered on the little bluff overlooking Huron for no longer than two minutes but took in a scene that moved me all day: the last lingering violet storm clouds from the previous evening, stripes of pale orange light between them and, most of all, the reflective waters, unhurriedly dabbing at the shore.

I had never heard of the Canadian poet William Wilfred Campbell (at this age, I have to qualify that by saying 'to the best of my recollection') until last Saturday. Looking for a poem about Huron to post on my blog along with sunrise photographs, I googled and came upon his *By Huron's Shore* with:

How I long for dawns in-blowing,
For the day-bloom, ruddier growing,
Into morning's perfect flower;
Watched in sweet, wind rustled hour,
*   Spirit-wrapt, by Huron's shore*
Where the stars die out like tapers…

I learned about him what little you can in a brief online search: that he spent the formative years of his youth in little Wiarton, Ontario, that he wrote affectionately in remembrance of sharing campfires "on the shingly beach of some lone lake shore," that he was intensely religious and saw God in creation, that he had a crisis of faith, and that he was dubbed "laureate of the lakes." Even in my brief reading I sensed a lonely spirit both exalted and humbled by the lake country.

I want to learn more about him and his love of our lake.

22

June 21, 2017

Huron is unknown and thus wilder in some ways than the Great Lake usually characterized that way, Superior. It has the greatest cumulative shoreline of any Great Lake because it contains thousands of islands – approximately 30,000 of the 35,000 in the Lakes. Among those islands are hundreds of private coves and passages that few know and few enter twice.

Looking out over Huron, I see the grace of being unknown. There is less likelihood of an attack in the name of resource development. Huron will remain largely as it is, into the mid-century.

That is, unless Ontario acts on a proposal to build a deep geologic repository for radioactive waste on its Huron shore.

June 22, 2017

In my first book I wrote a few lines about iconic conservationist Aldo Leopold's childhood seasons in the Les Cheneaux Islands, at the opposite end of Lake Huron. Marquette Island is unknown to me but I speculate (without much risk) that his time there was instrumental in his emotional education with regard to nature. The land ethic grew in part from the waters of the Great Lakes.

June 23, 2017

Like the *Harbour Fountain* before them, two tankers have been anchored several miles today. One is the *Bro Alma*, which flies under the flag of Singapore, is an oil/chemical tanker, has a gross tonnage of 12162 and was built in 2008. It's presumably a little early to receive its cargo from Dow Sarnia or another member of Chemical Valley.

The sun glinted off the two vessels this evening, giving them a romantic air, but I thought of what they and their oceangoing companions have done to the Great Lakes. The vessels, and the surfaces of the Lakes themselves, appear as benign as ever, while below the water line disruption is the norm – disruption they helped cause by transporting aquatic creatures in their ballast water from ports in Eurasia to our ports. Until flushing and exchange of ballast in salt water became a legal requirement a decade ago, the oceangoers were introducing an alien species annually, it seemed.

The most disruptive appears to have been the quagga mussel. *"Dreissena rostriformis bugensis* is indigenous to the Dneiper River drainage of Ukraine and Ponto-Caspian Sea," according to the U.S. Geological Survey. In 1991, it showed up in Lake Erie. It has infiltrated all five Great Lakes, but its greatest impact is in Lake Huron-Michigan. It can survive at depths far greater than its predecessor invasive mollusk, the zebra mussel.

Again, the USGS: "Quaggas are prodigious water filterers, removing substantial amounts of phytoplankton and suspended particulate from the water. As such, their impacts are similar to those of the zebra mussel. By removing the phytoplankton, quaggas in turn decrease the food source for zooplankton, therefore altering the food web." Translation: quagga and zebra mussels alter the food supply for the top predators, including the prized (and also nonnative) salmon, in unpredictable ways. But it seems now they are causing a salmon crash. You wouldn't know any of this by looking at the tankers, or the lakes from shore.

Of course, the shippers said for 15 years that strict ballast controls would cripple the industry economically. They haven't – any more than modern environmental laws killed off American industry in the 1970s. No matter how many times polluters cry wolf, people will believe them, especially people who hold elective offices and need lobbyist campaign contributions.

Complexity seems increasingly difficult for people to grasp. When the generalist looks into one of the Great Lakes and sees remarkably clear water, try telling him or her it's a bad thing. But in many areas of the system it is, because it signals the presence of many filterers hard at work doing what they do naturally, and upsetting the fish assemblage people want. What lies beneath is to the surface of the lakes as a computer program is to an abacus.

It is night now and the lights of the *Bro Alma* no longer glitter directly out on the lake. The unromantic thing to do, I do: and the marine traffic website shows the vessel docked in Sarnia. There it is impossible to dodge a visible truth: the city's Chemical Valley smolders and smokes and smells. But that is a sacrifice zone. Ordinarily we wouldn't tolerate such filth.

I wonder whether any of the gains we've made in environmental quality will hold, as long as the surface appears unvexed.

June 24, 2017

It has always bothered me that we will do things for shipwrecks that we won't do for sustenance. Well up the Huron shore we have the Thunder Bay National Marine Sanctuary near Alpena. It was the first such sanctuary in the U.S. waters of the Great Lakes and its impetus is the underwater fleet of more than 100 ships "from an 1844 sidewheel steamer to a modern 500-foot-long German freighter."

Now, I like shipwrecks (even though they're often attached to stories of death and great suffering) and read books about them obsessively for a time in high school. But more than artifacts of man are found underwater and many of them need protection from man: lake sturgeon spawning habitat, for example. But there is no market for sanctuaries organized around them.

Sadly, practical reasons exist. To attract community support the federal government says shipwreck sanctuaries promote tourism. Their glass-bottom boat rides are a source of oohs and ahs. Would there be tourism organized around fish habitat?

It comes down to human attitudes, and we're not evolved yet for mass fascination with spawning beds – yet fish communities contribute to human survival.

For years I've been talking up the idea of protected aquatic areas and protecting unspoiled Great Lakes islands. I hope to see one before I go.

Which leads to another quixotic cause – the idea of declaring the waters of the Great Lakes within U.S. boundaries, or at least the highest quality waters of Lake Superior and Huron, a park. Canada has created a National Marine Conservation Area spanning much of Superior. Why should the US not rise to this level? Protecting what we've got is just as important as cleaning up what we fouled. But selling the idea to people is unexpectedly difficult. There's the usual opposition organized around fears of barring economically lucrative industries, and the people I would expect to be allies simply don't think it's important.

One of my favorite Michigan laws, passed a century ago, touches on this theme: "All of the swamp or submerged lands lying along the borders of Lakes Erie, Huron, Michigan, Superior, and St. Clair…and also all swamp or submerged lands adjoining these lakes, or in the bayous adjoining or emptying into these lakes, and also all swamp or submerged lands contiguous to and lying along the shores of the Kalamazoo river, Grand river, and Muskegon river, which now belong to the state, or to which the state later acquires title, are set apart and dedicated for a public shooting and hunting ground, for the benefit and enjoyment of the people of the state. This park shall extend to the state line into the respective lakes from the shoreline of the lakes, and the outer boundary of the park shall be the center line of the lakes or the boundary of the state."

Shooting is the reason – public access and ownership is the implication.

Evening – Fitz and I paid a brief evening visit to the beach just now – not much of a beach, just a shrinking apron of sand and gravel. It's a pleasant night, but unremarkable, you might say – just the sloshing of chill blue waters, a clearing azure sky, a fresh breeze, an open horizon. It's unremarkable only if you become numb to wonder. And if you do, there's a remedy: stop and look and listen.

June 25, 2017

I should heed my own advice. It's only honest to say I am occasionally numb to wonder and the lake. I need to stop and pay attention.

A friend stopped by today and as an inlander reawakened my appreciation of the lake. She exclaimed over its beauty and was the reason we sat on landlord Debbie's patio for two hours overlooking Huron. The sound of waves washing the shore was calming. Freighters crept past. The sun peeked out occasionally. The pleasures were simple.

After we went inside, my friend engaged me in conversation about the state of her soul. She lamented her fatigue. She also mentioned a coincidence involving pearls, which we both interpreted as a sign of hope. I told her to look out for a perhaps subtle manifestation of a turning point in her life.

I think I will look to the lake for my direction. When I think of it I feel a benign presence and a comforting sense of my insignificance.

June 26, 2017

It was an unsettled day. I never felt organized or in charge of my own plan of action. The few times I stepped outside with Fitz and viewed the lake helped only a little. But just now at around 9, we wandered down to a shore abandoned by other humans and left to nearly placid waters and top heavy, degraded thunderclouds. I love that scene, this place and the feelings inspired so much that I am increasingly resistant to moving.

I have a scheme, probably the appropriate term, to persuade Debbie to let me stay at half rent, at least until she finds a full-time renter. I don't want to give up my lake.

I spend a considerable amount of time romanticizing the public. The love of citizens for the Great Lakes will save them, I like to think. But why do I believe that? Citizens put a deranged narcissist in the White House. People don't want to think, or know something new. They already know.

June 27, 2017

The idea that Huron is an overlooked or forgotten lake has even seeped into our government. At least one report issued by the Michigan Department of Environmental Quality poses the question whether Huron is a victim of amnesia. It's not the biggest Great Lake, the dirtiest, the most populated or the purest. It's just unlike any other lake on earth.

It's probably most forgotten because relatively few people surround it and therefore are closely associated with it. If there were such a statistic as person-hours of remembering, Huron would score low.

Even the most spectacular features of Huron can be easy to overlook. Twenty years ago, I spent considerable time with a friend searching for the dwarf lake iris. An exquisite miniature, it grows in all the world primarily on the shores of northern Lower Michigan and richly deserves its title as the official state wildflower.

It needs Huron and the cool, moist lakeshore air, and sand or thin soil over limestone-rich gravel or bedrock. Like any plant or animal whose prime habitat is the shoreline, the subtle dwarf lake iris is threatened.

June 28, 2017

Anchored out there several miles tonight is the *Edznard Schulte*, flying under the flag of the United Kingdom. Waiting to be summoned to Sarnia's Chemical Valley. I'm reminded of a Port Huron booster book I encountered in the local library, dating back to perhaps the 1950s describing the twinkling of the chemical towers and the nighttime flaring of gas as a beautiful tourist attraction.

June 29, 2017

I've scarcely seen the lake today. Pinned to my desk by work and apathy, I have spent no more than a few seconds at the water's edge – yet enough so that when I turned away from viewing the lake and simply listened, I was put in mind of a someone splashing herself or himself in a bathtub. A pleasing, cleansing sound. It's easy to forget water is the universal solvent. It can break down anything.

One of the discoveries Tom and I made in trips up the Huron shore is White Rock – not the village, but the rock itself. A few hundred yards offshore near Harbor Beach, it was once a monumental landmark. Henry Schoolcraft, who traveled in the region in 1820, called it "an enormous detached mass of transition limestone standing in the lake at the distance of half a mile from the shore. This is an object looked upon as a kind of milestone by the voyageurs and is known to all canoe and boat travelers of the region." It had enough prominence to figure as a boundary point in an 1807 treaty between the U.S. and the Ottawa, Chippewa, Wyandotte, and Potawatomi Indians.

It was sacred to the aboriginals, so how tragically fitting that the Air Force used it for target practice in the 1940s, hastening its erosion. A plaque on a bluff overlooking the lake observes, "Freshly killed game and other choice food was placed on the White Rock so the Great Spirit, Gitchi Manitou, would know the Anishinabeg were thankful for the gifts received from the natural environment." Today, like the promises made to those peoples, the rock is shrunken. I wasn't sure whether I saw it or just a grayish reflection off the water.

June 30, 2017

It was a classic June day. Reminiscent of carefree childhood times, the day dawned summer, light filtering through haze as well as the leaves of the back yard trees. In afternoon when Fitz and I visited the beach several times, the pale blue waters slurped against the shore. The wind subsided almost completely as the surf rolled in lazily. I captured a fine video, from the perspective between the twin pillars of Debbie's patio-bordering pine. Unthreatening rill after rill moved shoreward. Out farther, jet skis, kayaks and a motorboat variously traveled the water surface. I just wanted to give myself over to it.

Tonight around 10 I took Fitz down to the beach and saw several displays of fireworks in the deep distance beyond the water. O Canada! In these days of American government menace, I find some reassurance that we share this lake with a nation of equal concern for environmental stewardship and a benign government. We count on thee. But there was something poignant about those far off soundlessly exploding lights, something forlorn, like a receding hope.

With the holiday here and vacationers flooding the community, it is just now becoming visceral, as opposed to abstract, how different is the feeling when this place is an escape rather than home. The eyes see more clearly, the lungs breathe more deeply, and the spirit rises more loftily when you are a guest.

JULY

"Lake Huron Wind Leaves Carnage." That was the somewhat overstated headline in this morning's newspaper.

July 1, 2017

2017 is halfway through its life. And it is Canada Day. It's a good day for the public to remember the Great Lakes are not "ours," as in American. Looking up facts and figures this morning, I found something I should have known: the Great Lake with the largest Canadian surface area is Huron. I assumed it was Superior but the international boundary in that lake was drawn to Canada's disadvantage. I was reminded also that Georgian Bay alone is large enough to be among the world's 20 largest lakes.

I traversed a fertile field of statistics. 18-21% of the world's surface freshwater. Enough water to spread over the 48 contiguous states to a depth of 9.5 feet. Only 1% of the volume renewed annually. It's good for Power Point presentations, but it doesn't capture the glory.

I sat on Debbie's side porch chatting with her at mid-morning. We had both barely bothered to put on presentable clothes. I mentioned Canada Day but our conversation easily wandered like a slow river. Meanwhile, the lake was peopled with jet skis and small motorboats, the water colored like mercury.

This is lake cottage weekend. The common space landward of the two rows of cottages is occupied by more vehicles than I have seen before. There is little room for any additional metal. The atmosphere is festive down by the lake. Unfortunately, the Fourth of July revelers have brought several dogs and separating them from Fitz means restraining him from the beach. I plan to pay my respects to Huron at dusk.

Later – it's after dusk and I'm still waiting. The informal neighborhood fireworks display continues. More sound than light. I'd like to take my drink of lake in peace.

31

July 2, 2017

Of light and the lake:

- I took Fitz down to the beach last night around 11. The waxing moon was high in the west and shone over our shoulders like an interested observer. The lake seemed a little breathless, hurrying against the shore. Perhaps rare immigrants from Canada sneaking in under the poor cover of a moonlit night. Two sets of lights, one barely visible to the north, marked freighters. Still, humanity was little evident.
- At the same spot at 8:30 this morning, the radiance was powerful, illuminating the footprints and flotsam invisible last night. How forgiving the darkness can be. Fitz leaped the narrow creek mouth in search of beach riches for his sense of smell.

I came to and went from the beach all afternoon as friends hosted a pot luck. Neighborhood residents and vacationers clogged the little strip of sand. Until the sky turned gray, boats crisscrossed the lazy waters. High summer.

As was true last night, neighbors and their guests set off a cannonade of fireworks around dusk, launching from the beach. I wonder whether anyone on the entire Michigan shore who was engaged in fireworks paused to celebrate mentally the existence of the lakes he or she stood beside. More indestructible, I hope, than the Declaration or the Constitution.

July 3, 2017

On how many summer days will Lake Huron be as deep a blue as this? Air and water in their own ways are cleansed today – the air, dried and purged of pollutants by a northern air mass and the water stirred by a northeast wind. The light is more brilliant, the cool more pleasantly chill, all feelings and thoughts thrown into sharp relief by the clear delineation of land, water, and air.

Tonight – as the sky turned pale after sunset, the lake happily jiggled as it turned gray. The buoys winked green, the Canadian wind turbines blinked red on the far shore.

I began one of my Great Lakes books with a parable about the ecosystem degraded by climate change and diversion, the air warming and the water drying up to the point where freighters can no longer traverse Lake St. Clair without the help of a major engineering project. A family spends part of a day enjoying a kind of ecotourism, learning about the former grandeur of the Great Lakes. In writing it I bought into the assumption that climate change would mean hotter, dryer weather in the Great Lakes. In fact, I dated the beginning of plummeting lake levels at 2016. But Erie and Ontario are near or above record highs.

I don't regret the idea of a parable, but I do regret not capturing the uncertainty of a complicated global phenomenon affecting a complex aquatic ecosystem. The parable reads like an overlong, exaggerated bedtime story.

July 4, 2017

For the second straight year, I attended the neighborhood 4th of July celebration, a true piece of uniquely American patriotism. It took place on a wide lawn overlooking the glistening lake, outside a dwelling more accurately described as a manor.

First, the setting. The unrelenting sun exacted a toll in heat until the east wind picked up. The lake was choppy but without whitecaps. The panorama was sprawling; no shrubs, trees or even fences interfered with the view. Canada was vivid to the southeast, not the phantom of humid or overcast weather.

The program was the same as last year's and probably close to what it has been for 33 years: the raising of a mammoth American flag accompanied by a recording of the national anthem; a recording of *The Ragged Old Flag* by Johnny Cash and a recording of John Wayne's Fourth of July tribute; an acknowledgment of veterans in the group, neighborhood residents who passed away over the last year, and newborns (mostly grandkids); and a ritual involving kids putting their hands on the flag. Two things pleasantly surprised me: the raising of the Canadian flag and the playing of that nation's anthem; and what I interpreted as a disparaging remark about Trump by the emcee. I had just assumed this neighborhood was Trump land.

After the program, which took perhaps 45 minutes, a serve-yourself buffet of carbohydrates was offered and neighbors reintroduced themselves. Debbie said hi to several she sees once a year, at this gathering.

It's difficult not to worry about this nation right now. Looking out over that water, one wonders what shape it would be in had the current regime ruled in 1970. I doubt it would sparkle. But there are even graver concerns.

Later -- the lake facing window and screen door are open to the wind. And the sound of the waves. I could sit here every summer evening and listen and feel and let my life slowly unwind. Maybe that's the way it will go. It's not the end I envisioned 40 years ago. I wanted to be great but after all I'm deeply and immutably flawed. I owned a lot of false pride then. Even today I possess a kind of intractable arrogance masked by a humble demeanor. As I get closer to the lake, it might level that out. The lake isn't humble or arrogant but beyond those things.

I wrote the other day that only a visitor can see the glory of the lake with fresh eyes. Another overstatement. In any relationship affection and appreciation come and go. I will get it back, as long as I am open to it. But if I have my eye on a screen or my mind on an abstraction it will deflect off me.

July 6, 2017

I have spent the last two nights in the magnificent house of friends near on the Lake Michigan shore of the Leelanau Peninsula. High on a bluff that on clear days commands stirring views of the Manitou and Fox Islands, their vantage point has also yielded glimpses of shadow-laced evening waters 80 feet below spreading out for dozens of square miles. It's a significantly different experience from the Port Huron view but each has charms. It's also all one lake, after all.

I watched the sun rise before six over Huron and set after 9:30 over Michigan yesterday.

July 8, 2017

My friend took me on a walk in the early morning and one in the evening Thursday. One ended in a half mile of cobblestone beach walking, or tottering. The route of the other, its south end contiguous with the north end of the first, traversed mostly sand. He says they sometimes flip from sand to rock and vice versa. Neither of us knows why or has seen anything like it before.

The other clear impression of the walks was the ever-rising lake level. He said 20-foot high foredunes and an interdunal pond from even two years ago are gone.

Walking with these friends along the shore in the evening, I was struck by the intense brightness of the 8 p.m. light. We were on a floodlit stage bordered by ceaseless surf.

Late morning – from Lake Huron.

The *Bro Alma* is back, anchored offshore waiting for the "come home" call from its Sarnia mom.

A northeast wind has risen again. I could hear it whipping up froth last night but it was 12 hours after returning from Traverse City before I got down to the water. That water has invaded the beach because of the wind direction, smoothing the sand and washing away the pebbles but further encroaching on suntan territory. There is little room to pitch a chair.

Evening – among those who have likened the shapes of islands on the horizon to vessels, I rank in the thousands. But that's how the Manitous looked from the beach at my friends' house this week. They and the Foxes were barely perceptible as gray lines in the thick, humid air. Like vessels in the distance, islands in the distance pique the romantic curiosity. What is out there? What would it feel like to be there?

I looked up the numbers. The Manitous, the Foxes and 722 others in Lake Michigan and over 35,000 islands throughout the Great Lakes are more than intrigue for the imagination. Isolated from many processes on the mainland, they are refuges for wildlife and especially plants.

They are "the world's largest collection of freshwater islands and contain significant biodiversity including endemic species, rare habitats and critical biological functions," Dave Ewert, a scientist I know, said at a conference in 2015. "They are important breeding and staging areas for colonial nesting waterbirds, harbour noteworthy assemblages of plants and animals and provide important stopover sites for migrating birds."

I have set foot on three Great Lakes islands not known for biological diversity: Mackinac (tourist lure), Belle Isle (Detroit playground) and Grosse Ile (urban footnote.)

35

Beaver Island, where I spoke for the Central Michigan University Biological Station, is different. It's the largest island in Lake Michigan and contains every major wetland type, a variety of forests and rare and endangered species like the Michigan Monkey-Flower, a yellow-petaled plant thought to be the only plant endemic to Michigan. Probably the island's most important biological value is its service as an emergency landing spot for birds migrating north in the spring. They can exhaust themselves in fog or fighting strong northern winds but the island helps save them.

One of my Great Lakes fights was over a proposed development of North Fox Island in the early 1990s. It took a while and was nasty at times but in the end the state bought all 848 acres. I was fighting more over the idea of the island than the reality of it. I doubt I'll ever set foot on it.

July 9, 2017

Late morning -- Fitz and I strolled out back just now. A family of six, with all 4 kids looking 10 or under, is using the commons. One of the girls is wearing water wings. They seem happy enough. I wonder if I should warn them about the creek, which Debbie says conveys farm waste. I have no proof of that.

Docked offshore are:
- The *Arneborg*, under the flag of The Netherlands.
- The *Bro Alma*, still waiting, now for more than a day.

Traveling south at 10 knots into the St. Clair River is *The Grand Illusion*.

Evening – the air is heavy and like the lake is still. A half hour ago a last powerboat was racing from out in the open lake back to Port Huron or Sarnia. The parked freighters are gone. The weekend is over.

July 10, 2017

Some docks in Georgian Bay almost cost the US treasury several billion dollars. The docks belong to influential Canadian politicians who were dismayed, like many full-time residents, when the level of Georgian Bay fell so low that water barely reached the dock.

The Canadian government was not going to spend many billions of its own dollars to improve access. Instead the Canadian government came to the

IJC and asked for a resolution endorsing the construction of underwater structures, informally dubbed "speed bumps," in the St. Clair River to hold back Lake Huron water and by that means raise the water level of Georgian Bay. By a 5-1 vote the Commission approved the resolution, but the US State Department rejected it out of hand.

Beyond showing how one country's set of politicians may try to influence politics on the other side, this shows how the far reaches of a Great Lake are all connected. Georgian Bay residents have a vital interest in what's happening a few miles south of here.

July 11, 2017

Heading north of Fort Gratiot this evening on M-25, the Huron coast road, I passed a spot that reminds me of northern Michigan. It's a roadside park on a bluff overlooking a broad vista of Huron. The bluff setting is comparable to those west of St. Ignace on US-2. A birch tree or two adds to the northern flair. It is rare on the Huron shore for the public to have access to such scenery. There is probably plenty of it, but nearly the entire shore from Port Huron to Port Austin is in private hands. That's regrettable, because a view like the one I saw tonight relaxes the soul.

I'm increasingly convinced I want to retain a foothold on Huron. I might even write a book about it.

July 12, 2017

The lighthouse cult. I encountered it while looking up something else on the internet. The article featured the half dozen lighthouses of the Thumb. People accumulate Great Lakes lighthouses like birders build a life list. I like lighthouses – they are inspiring and reassuring in a storm. I can't, however, fathom collecting memorabilia associated with them and striving to see all of them. Especially if you don't care about the quality of the water over which they stand guard.

Later – I return to the thought that there's something wild and almost desperate about Huron. Its obscurity enables me to interpret it in any number of ways. I find it most ominous in the dark nights of winter when, standing on the shore, I look out onto wan patches of ice scattered over black waters under a menacingly gray-black sky. Huron is of course indifferent to me but in those moments it feels malevolent.

July 13, 2007

After 35 years of working on environmental policy, I should know a lot more than I do about some things. Like what rights the public has to the shoreline. When I moved here, I was circumspect about walking the neighbors' beaches. I knew I had some rights to pass along the water's edge but I wasn't confident enough in my knowledge to act on it.

Instead of looking up the answer in an authoritative guide I acted the part of the sheep and looked around to see what others did. Neighbor Ken just hoofed the beach with his feisty dog Mojo. Rachel, the dog sitter, said the public had rights to the first 10 feet and that's where she walked Fitz.

Then I asked Jim Olson, a friend then and also a colleague now, and he told me what I knew but didn't know I knew, based on the linchpin of my master's thesis, the public trust doctrine. In 2005 the Michigan Supreme Court ruled in favor of the public's right to shoreline access, shocking observers of that conservative court and displeasing lakefront property owners.

But what is the "ordinary high-water mark" that divides private from public? The court gave close to a "you'll know it when you see it" definition. Which means there will be more litigation. I do, however, walk the beach with Fitz with greater confidence. Or did, until the lake recently came very close to the ordinary high-water mark and blocked the way to the south unless I was willing to get wet up to the top of the ankle while soaking Fitz.

July 14, 2017

In the unflinching morning sunlight glaring off the water, Fitz and I encountered the corpse of a gull. A trivial moment in the history of the lake or even this beach, but the death of any recognizable being always inspires soul-searching. Did this bird have consciousness, feel love, understand its imminent death? Did it feel pain as it died? Did it matter or was it just a fraction of the world's biomass? There are no definitive answers to these questions any more than there is a voice that responds to prayers to God. It's part of the great chasm between our world and the next. If there is one.

The gull lay on its side as if sleeping and the waves expertly re-sorted the sand around it. It appeared possible the corpse would be captured by the lake and on a return trip this afternoon it was gone, just as was the sputtering flame of consciousness that had preceded its death.

July 15, 2017

Fitz and I spent the morning running errands – laundromat, coffee shop, pet store. We were a mile inland. Which had me wondering again why anyone in a region like this chooses to live anywhere farther from the big water than a mile or so. It's like living next door to a world-class live theater but never having the money to buy a ticket and get inside. You might as well live 50 miles away.

Which led to another thought – shoreline access. I have never seen so few opportunities for the public to approach one of the Great Lakes as I have in the Thumb Coast. Nearly 70 miles, from Lakeport to west of Port Austin, lacks a state park. A few scenic turnouts and tiny township parks are the sole opportunities for visitors to approach the lake (the Harbor of Refuge at Harbor Beach is a big exception).

As I was musing a few weeks ago, the development of this region of Michigan is so unlike that on the west shore and I think the difference can be traced in part to money and class. Prosperous Chicagoans have made their summers on the west Michigan coast for decades and their influence has been felt in preservation battles. The unionized working class of southeast Michigan colonized this part of the Huron shore and with limited funds for leisure built modest cottages and cabins. To make a second mortgage affordable it was necessary to subdivide the shoreline into tiny slivers -- very many of them – blocking public shore access. The public is deprived of its heritage.

Evening – one of the cheering features of summer is a weekend regatta out of the Sarnia Yacht Club. On a weekend afternoon 20 or 30 sailboats in the distance silently vie for position, coming out perhaps two miles before rounding a buoy and returning home. Like tidy teeth, the triangular white sails efficiently cut through the water. It's so inconsequential but so much effort goes into these races. The lake is a superb playground on mild sun engulfed days. You wouldn't know how punishing it can be in the fall.

July 16, 2017

How much is a view worth? This morning I visited Debbie, who has an awful cold, and we got to discussing the idea of her renting out her place in the summer and fall. She has a million-dollar view of Huron from what she calls her front deck, but we settled on $1500 a week. It sounded as though she's never considered renting to tourists.

Today is Lake Superior Day. Worthy of celebration she is. But Superior has struck me as too big and cold to love – admire and respect, yes, but not love. As the forgotten lake, Huron has a bigger claim on my love.

Because I'll be out of town Friday and Saturday, I'll miss a local tradition, the Port Huron to Mackinac sailboat race. Or as it's now known, the Bell's Beer Bayview Mackinac race. Several hundred craft sail either a 204-mile or 259-mile course. But the real action, I hear, is the night before in downtown Port Huron, when the crews turn a big profit for local bar owners.

I delayed departure on a trip last year to watch one of the clusters set off from the buoy directly offshore. It was a disappointment. Even with binoculars the boats were little more than insect size.

July 17, 2017

This morning's memory is poignant. I'm sitting in a motel in Traverse City, but 17 hours ago I took Fitz down to the beach not long after sunrise. The sky was overcast but for a hole punched into the gray armor to the northeast. The lake was subsiding after a thunderous night, but still muttered its discontent. Fitz and I were one of a few – maybe the only – creatures to observe all of it in just this way.

July 21, 2017

Since Wednesday evening, I've been only a little farther from the Gulf coast than I am from Lake Huron when I'm at home. Until you get a whiff of salt air or step in the biologically rich water, you can imagine you are on the doorstep of one of the Great Lakes.

Last night we took in the sunset. Nothing remarkable in itself but combined with the extraordinary sky it was an unforgettable scene. Several lines of towering clouds bracketed the heavens – in a display whose rival I don't remember and it may not exist. Finely etched, these titans advanced in various directions like a military band breaking into sections on a playing field. We saw a rabbit on its haunches, a dog and a helmeted warrior shape in the clouds.

This is all about the sky, but this sky wouldn't be accessible without the water, just like the spectacular sunrises of my home would not be approachable without Huron. They are a partnership of startling beauty.

I admire the beach, water and sky wherever they may be found together. But I adore Huron.

July 24, 2017

After nearly a week away from the lake, I returned late this afternoon and instead of going to it and seeking comfort, I plunged almost immediately into the business of email and document editing. The state is holding a meeting tomorrow night in Traverse City about what to do regarding the rickety oil pipeline in the Straits of Mackinac. My group is rightly in favor of removing the pipeline, so we were preparing comments to make at the meeting and an accompanying news release. This proves again that some environmental advocates are among the Americans most divorced from the outdoors. We're too busy being inside in research and meetings.

I took a break and went to the gym. When I returned a front was running through town, its cloud fingers reaching down menacingly toward the lake. I did race down to the water then to take a photo, which didn't capture the drama of the fast-moving front. The lake was running from north to south with plenty of whitecaps. Even now, after midnight, I can hear it thundering.

Afternoon – the weather service posted a beach hazard warning today, something more characteristic of the other three seasons. It was warranted. The northeast wind is strong and steady. Waves are five to six feet high and the beach is engulfed. It's not safe to let Fitz get anywhere near water's edge as rogue waves occasionally wash up near the higher ground. Not safe (or comfortable) for freighters either, apparently. I haven't seen one all day.

Evening – well, I saw one tonight and the waves are no less menacing. I can only guess that it is relatively calmer away from the shore. This wave storm seems to be the result of the lake hurling itself against the land.

Meanwhile, I have been struggling to draft a letter to the Trump Administration, on behalf of FLOW, defending the boundaries of the Thunder Bay National Marine Sanctuary in northern Lake Huron. The Administration is apparently acting at the behest of the oil, mining and coal lobby to trim the size of national monuments and sanctuaries to permit exploration and development. I've written a few hundred letters like this in my career and recognize their necessity. But I also recognize that this letter will affect the decision not one whit. Other considerations that dangle price tags will be more influential.

July 25, 2017

The waves of the last two days have been so strong and insistent that they have again plugged up the creek that runs behind this cottage. The lake piled up a dam of sand at the creek mouth. It's a sturdy dam and will take a day or two to break. I haven't seen this phenomenon quite so robust. At times, the wind has driven the lake up the creek like an estuary, but it hasn't often blocked it off. The benefit is that, for a couple of days, the lake will suffer one less source of sediment.

I was able to speak up for Lake Huron on Twitter the other day. (Big accomplishment.) The person who tweets as Lake Superior inspired someone to tweet that there are four good lakes, but only Superior is a Great Lake. Rather than challenge that, I declared Huron the underrated lake. It felt right, but perhaps that's because I underrated it until two years ago. Much of the Great Lakes community has joined me.

Every now and then I reflect on the proposal to site the deep geologic repository for low- and medium-level radioactive waste on the opposite side of the lake, about 70 miles from here in Ontario. It's characteristic of so many Great Lakes issues. The proponent declares that technology will minimize any risk to a vanishingly low level. The many opponents, animated by their passion for the Lakes, sometimes also armed with science, rely on common sense. Why take even a slight risk with the largest freshwater system in the world? Especially with radioactive materials that could remain lethal for tens or hundreds of thousands of years.

But these threats and this logic appear with such frequency that the latter is discounted. The official governmental decisionmaking process pivots on technical specifics but typically rejects simple logic – and the passion. That puts the Great Lakes at a disadvantage.

When I sit on the communal bench out back overlooking Lake Huron, though, the passion and the logic assume dominance, and I can't fathom why even a supposedly foolproof and failproof technology is tolerated close to the Great Lakes when the consequences of failure would be grave.

42

July 26, 2017

"Lake Huron Wind Leaves Carnage." That was the somewhat overstated headline in this morning's *Times Herald*. It was sufficiently alarming to entice Debbie to come out from town and look for damage to her property.

There was none, but to the north it was different. Donna of Worth Township suffered a smashed boat hoist, and on the shore just north of Fort Gratiot damage was done to boat, jet skis, hoists and docks. Property owners there said the strongest waves were concentrated on their neighborhood. Winds were clocked up to 40 knots and waves were guesstimated as peaking at 10 feet.

My favorite part of the article has to do with the local weather lore. Diana was waiting for a "little nor'easter" to hit at the end of June or early July, but it came three weeks late. She described it as an annual event.

In truth, it seems an unusual year. Daylong, vigorous north to northeast winds have arisen four or five times since winter. They have turned the lake an angry gray-green.

Back at this place, Debbie expressed relief at escaping harm (although the lake left a calling card of pebbles and vegetation at the fringe of her patio five feet above the water). She recalled again the ice boulders that rolled up nearly to the door to the house her first winter here, 1986.

If I needed a reminder of the destructive power of the Great Lakes, it came in an email from my cousin. She was reviewing a summary of her thoughts on the Lakes that I had composed for a book. In it, she had described the loss, during her childhood, of friends' fathers in a boating accident in Lake Michigan. Today she proposed I add this:

"In all, 8 children were fatherless after that night. It was a very long couple of days waiting for the bodies to be recovered and the funerals to be held. It wasn't a memory I will ever forget. To this day, chills run down my spine when I think of that terrible storm and the many lives impacted by Lake Michigan. I will never forget the fact that the Lake can turn from a quiet calm body of beautiful water to a place of surging waves and death."

July 27, 2017

The bullfrog appears to like the plugged-up creek. He has relocated with his banjo to the dam at what once was the outlet to the lake. He strums a note every 10 or 20 minutes.

A piece I wrote for *Traverse the Magazine* went on line today. Entitled "We Unite Over Water," its essence is this quote: "As the right and left, the Republican and Democratic Parties, the environmentalists and the developers clash over almost everything—and often bitterly—I've seen quantitative and qualitative evidence that water washes away much of that rancor. Water, in short, is something people of all kinds want to protect."

An hour later I saw an article about the Republican Congressional attempt to undermine further the Obama clean water rule.

I want to believe my thesis. I'm not sure I do.

July 28, 2017

The lake is raging tonight. A day and a half after the last nor'easter died down, the wind backed into the northeast again and the whitecaps began to build last evening. The fierce crashing surf has persisted all day and now, at 10:30 p.m., is as loud as ever. I've left the deck door open with only the fine mesh of the screen door trying to interfere with the strong wind entering.

It's easy to see – and hear – why observers liken storm-thrashed lakes to angry gods. The restlessness of the lake spilling over its beaches is reminiscent of a person trying to burst his or her bonds.

July 29, 2017

I performed my rite, the occasional toe dip, this morning. The lake seemed colder again. I had no desire to go farther. Nor would it have been safe. The waves keep punishing the shore. For a while a month ago I occasionally heard a sound like a screen door slamming. Today the source of that sound as I expected was confirmed. Debbie said a part of the jetty is rattling. She never heard the sound before, but the combination of the jetty's age and constant storms is wearing the jetty out.

It's only honest to say the din of these waves is growing tiresome.

For a while I've wanted to produce a comparison of the amount of water in the Great Lakes with something else that holds water to help make

44

understandable the vastness of the lakes. I've done hand calculations and used a calculating machine and software, but have been unable to get an answer I trust. So just now in desperation I asked my smartphone's Siri. Dividing 6 quadrillion gallons by the 660,000 gallons in an Olympic-sized pool, she came up with 9,090,909,090.909. That's the number of pools that the Great Lakes could fill. I don't think that helps much.

July 30, 2017

Tom took the lake's temperature before leaving at noon – 74 degrees. Tepid, for Huron. It was a perfect day for a swim but he had to depart before he could do so in order to get to work by 3. In contrast, he had all day yesterday available, but five-foot waves and a chill breeze discouraged that.

He had news of his favorite spot on the beach at the state park – it's underwater. He said the entire park beach is submerged except for an apron below the bath houses. We know it's part of a cycle, but if the water gets higher government will try to make a difference, however feebly, with cash payments or low interest loans to affected landowners to move houses. But building or buying too close to the precipice should carry some consequences.

July 31, 2017

I arrived at a decision today that in some ways I'd already made – to hang on to the cottage a couple of months after I move to Traverse City. I just can't say goodbye to it, especially because of the lake. As I backed out of the driveway yesterday and paused, I glimpsed between two of the neighborhood homes an indistinct hot line of blue, the line of summer. How, I wondered, could I abandon it? I will take a hit financially but it's worth it.

I received by email a friend's photo of the bright green Lake Erie water out back of her house south of Monroe yesterday, and posted it on Twitter. It excited some interest as the western Lake Erie basin is expected to have an awful algal bloom in August. Erie is a victim of dead-end, toxic policy. The yeoman farmer is the fake symbol that the corporate farm lobby trots out to resist (successfully) effective pollution controls. We are so good at praising the Lakes with our words while condemning them with our actions.

Huron Lady II is the name of the little cruise ship that takes tourists boldly down the St. Clair River and meekly out a short distance into Huron. Tom wants to take one more trip with me. Yes! As the vessel slips under the Blue Water Bridge heading north you can almost feel the engine trying to shed all constraints and merge into the vastness.

AUGUST

Photographs associate themselves with memories over time. And I find photographs about Great Lakes summers become more poignant with years.

August 1, 2017

It's a truism that summers gallop past faster as you age. But now they're starting to stampede. August: at the same time that I accept the reality of it, I shudder in disbelief.

If this August is like the first two, the roar of the powerboats will contain a new urgency each weekend. Kids on the beach will be a little more high-pitched, perhaps as much in excitement about the new school year as sorrow about the dwindling away of summer. Sunrise over the lake will rapidly move forward to 6:45, meaning photography will resume. Purposeful birds will head south along the shore. And, if I retain a foothold here, I will look forward to the peace and solitude of the lake in winter.

The shadows of the tallest trees along the shore are already lengthening and appearing a little sooner than before. The cycle renews.

Tonight, I vow, well after dark, I will go down to the lake and say a prayer to the lake, not for me but for it.

August 2, 2017

At 11:45 pm. Fitz and I walked down to the beach. The lake had energy but was running in place, waves barely creasing the shore. In the glow of the flashlight, I saw a folding patio chair placed on the beach facing lakeward, and a stack of stones on the table beside. Two illuminated freighters, one faint like a distant planet, moved northward. I could hear the throbbing of the nearer vessel's engine even though it might have been five miles off. It may have been the *Algoway*. Meanwhile, the two nearby buoys blinked dumbly, and the moon looked down in confusion through a speckle cloud.

August 3, 2017

This morning was a summer whiteout over the lake – not snow, but the combination of a light fog and the glint of sunlight on the water. About an hour after Fitz and I visited the beach, a freighter sounded repeatedly, an ominous, mournful sound.

Tonight, the lake was like the last guest at a party, his back to the door, to realize a bad guy has entered. The lake offered a silver smile as a black storm cloud crept overhead.

I was reflecting on what it means when politicos boast that the Great Lakes hold 20% of the world's freshwater? It's more complicated than it sounds. That's 20% of the <u>surface</u> freshwater. There are vast stores of groundwater.

And the polar ice caps harbor a monumental amount of freshwater that climate change might be liberating. (When is a tycoon going to secure rights to capture the meltwater for profit?) So the correct formulation is 20% of the available surface freshwater in the world. Not too many politicians will pause to utter the qualifiers. And even with them, the Great Lakes are a lot of water.

At my lunch in Traverse City with a friend Tuesday, I mentioned how much I'm resisting the thought of leaving Lake Huron. He nodded knowingly and remarked that I was a wreck when I moved here but have found solace. I was surprised he knew about all that. It was like having a secret lover revealed.

August 4, 2017

When you're on the west shore of a lake and the prevailing winds are westerly, a tempest can be brewing, or thrashing the lake, and you have no idea. The nearshore is calm with a few riffles, and you're in a pocket of tranquility. This afternoon the sky quickly darkened and a breeze kicked up but from the shore it was difficult to discern any significant difference.

Late today FLOW filed two lengthy submittals with the State of Michigan regarding the pipelines at the Straits of Mackinac. They're 64 years old and poorly maintained by their owner, Enbridge. The risk of a catastrophic spill is great. A University of Michigan professor estimated that "nearly 60% of Lake Huron's open water (13,611 square miles) could be affected by visible oil from a spill in the Straits."

The entire staff and two volunteer experts poured hundreds of hours into the work and built an impressive case against continued operation of these menaces. I posted a short "shut it down" on my blog but I have no faith that the politicians will do so imminently. After three years of study they will call for more study.

I understand it although I don't like it. When I worked for the governor I became such a creature of the system that I crouched to withstand the winds of change rather than harnessing them. I remember one case where he and I were lifted by that wind. When I told him that the oil and gas interests would be angry about his work to keep drilling out of Nordhouse Dunes, he said, "Screw the oil companies." I wanted to cheer.

Why is it so often oil? I believe petroleum may be the root of all evil in American society. It stains our politics and blackens our ethical standards.

August 5, 2017

The waves have been rising all morning until they are pounding relentlessly at the jetties. They make a powerful sound, a slow, massive heaving like a monster's breast. In three hours, the lake has occupied most of the beach. Still, two guests whom I presume are from a neighbor's rental are sitting in folding lawn chairs, unperturbed, reading, just up from the beach on the small rise. More worrisome are the three kids from a couple of cottages north who have swum out 200 feet minus life jackets and are riding the mounting waves with kick boards.

Fitz and I go a mile inland to find a walking path and it's a different world. A modest breeze, hardly a lake-churner. But the angle over the water is just right to foster an assault on the shoreline.

Evening – with the deck door pulled back, it's easy to hear the surf, still strong, but diminished from early afternoon. My experience is that it will be audible all night. Listening to it from bed is like being rocked in the cradle.

Debbie has campers in her back yard – what she calls the front yard – overlooking the water. Friends of neighbors. They'll be cradled, all right. And rocked.

After midnight – the swells persist have but diminished further. Depending on your point of view, it is the sound of a tired man falling asleep or the agonal breath of the dying. Either way, it has a majesty beyond the human.

The bullfrogs are having an idiosyncratic chorus in the creek just outside the window. Or is it one hyperactive bullfrog? If so, he has recognized his imperative. It is August.

August 6, 2017

The lake was calm this morning. But the aftermath testified to the storm. The waves had gnawed at the beach, leaving gap-toothed fang marks with spaces of clean sand. They had also hurled small stones in wide zones at the foot of the beach.

Mixed in among the stones were a few zebra mussel shells. They've done their damage and aren't the scourge they were almost 30 years ago. Their legacy lives on in a disrupted Great Lakes food web.

Debbie and I swapped the usual Sunday morning sustenance – this week, a grande Starbuck's coffee from me, a muffin with scrambled eggs from her, a good deal for me – and talked the lake again. When we talk lake levels her mind always travels back to her first winter here and the storm that pitched ice boulders almost to her house. We also talked about how you sometimes must actively listen to notice the sound of surf. Like people living near a railroad track or highway – and I'm sorry to compare Huron to them – you adjust to the lake's voice and sometimes lose it as background. Although when it's thundering you can't ignore it.

A critic of FLOW's position on the Enbridge pipeline has shown up on my Facebook page. One of those who tutored me on Michigan environmentalism when I joined the community, he says among other things that federal law pre-empts the state's authority and therefore Michigan cannot close down or limit the pipeline much. It's a good test of the public trust doctrine. Enbridge can occupy the submerged lands under the Straits by virtue of permission from the state. Federal law should not be permitted to nullify a principle reaching back well over 1000 years for the convenience of a corporation today.

Fitz and I did a little beachcombing this evening. I have violated basic beach etiquette and sanitation by permitting him to relieve himself on the sand early in the morning and in the evening. I can't condone it. Yet I do it. Tonight, he emptied his bladder in the grass.

It was a lovely scene. Anchored just on the Canadian side of the border (according to marinetraffic.com), the *Algosea* turned on its lights. The lake was glassy under dramatic white clouds and took on their hue.

August 7, 2017

I'm sitting in Cadillac at 9:48 p.m. but I began the day on the lake. I took

Fitz down to the beach and we were present at the 6:27 sunrise time. But it was impossible to tell when the sun appeared. A blanket of clouds smothered it and even though there were openings in the overcast to the south, the exposed sky there remained drab. But the lake! It is often at its best when becalmed. The gentlest lapping reminded me of my dog stirring and stretching upon waking.

Feeling remorseful about letting Fitz use the beach as his bathroom, I looked up the issue of water pollution from dog waste and it is as serious as I thought. The average pile of dog poop contains 3 billion fecal coliform bacteria. As much as 90 percent of the fecal coliform in urban stormwater was of non-human origin, and most of this was from dogs. I hope by plucking his poop immediately off the stones or sand, I minimize the transfer.

From microorganisms to whales. When I began my career in the State Capitol I was told a legislator had requested a bill to introduce whales to the Great Lakes to promote tourism. Apparently, the lawmaker had to be told the whales do best in salt water.

August 8, 2017

Housed in the Traverse City FLOW office, I had little chance to feel or think about Huron today. But I can still see yesterday morning's calm at sunrise, the lake still dreaming of the day's potential. I want to dream that tomorrow.

August 10, 2017

Returning home about 11:30 p.m., I unpacked and walked down to the beach. It is a calm night but the lake is quietly agitated like a man stirring in his sleep. Coming around the corner of Debbie's house on my way to the beach, I was robbed of my breath by the sight of the busy lake crinkling in a column of light cast by the waning moon. The only other witness to this scene of ravishing beauty seemed to be a southbound freighter.

August 11, 2017

Fitz was happy to see me this morning, and I him, after four days apart. We celebrated by going down to the beach and sniffing around. I use that phrase deliberately. I metaphorically sniffed, looking for interesting beach debris below and cloud formations high over the lake.

While we were gone, somebody dug a trench in an attempt to reconnect the creek with the lake. They were successful in leaving a dry ditch. The amount of sand piled at the mouth of the creek is still enough to restrain the creek's flow.

It's probably my imagination, but the lake seems even higher today than it was last weekend. I peeked over the jetty to the south and the sloshing water seems to have risen against the seawall.

Last night's photographs of the shimmering waters under the moon turned out fairly well with considerable manipulation of the smart phone. One of my Facebook friends compared it to a Japanese wood block.

Late in the afternoon I took Fitz down to the county park. On this still, gray, drizzly day, the public had abandoned it. Only five or six cars dotted the parking lot. The lake was flat, lazy and colorless. The scene reminded me of early March or late November.

Evening--we went out back toward 7:30 PM and found the immediate shoreline peopled by visitors and residents. But the lake captured my eyes at once. A kayaker was traveling north to south, crossing my angle of view, against the backdrop of mammoth thunderclouds marching across Ontario. The clouds were so tall and so white in the reflected sunlight that their shine laid down a white road cross the lake. The kayaker crossed the road from curb to curb and continued.

Out of nowhere, waves slapped the shore before subsiding. An elderly couple sat with arms around each other on a bench in the backyard of the house to the north. Four or five elderly guests stood on the small beach to the south. Life continued as it does every August even as the TV 200 feet away screamed about looming nuclear war.
As I took in the same scene, I was again puzzled by the difference between the caring people have for the Great Lakes and the state of the lakes themselves. This degenerated into a bundle of unhappy laments.

A conservative whom I respect often spoke on the theme that a healthy economy is necessary to support environmental protection. In other words, we should not bridle the economy in the false pursuit of pristine air, water and land. My retort is that a healthy environment is necessary to support a robust economy. In other words, we need to have strong protections for the environment, sometimes costing businesses and taxpayers money, if we want to have a good economy. You can't go to work if you can't breathe.

I also reflected on the decline of civic participation. You often get the feeling if not the words from people that public policy is a lot of boring government stuff. And then suddenly a piece of legislation comes along to take away their health insurance and people realize it's not abstract. Nor is the air we breathe. Boring government stuff was once considered substantive entertainment worth studying and participating in. Now it can't compete with the reality shows that produce an illiterate president. One reason the Great Lakes are floundering is that people are not paying attention to boring government stuff. If the Lakes brim with algae and teem with invasive species, then it's not boring government stuff anymore.

August 12, 2017

Another sunrise over the lake missed. I just haven't had the mojo to arise and witness sunrises lately. I'm hoping tomorrow to resume the custom. It's been one of the most cherished rituals here for the last two years.

When we did finally arrive at the water's edge around 7:15, it was a summer white out again. I held my hand up to block the piercing reflection off the lake. The way you ward off mosquitoes. Not all about nature is bliss and beauty.

On the other hand, I'm sitting in front of a TV blaring the news about white racists demonstrating in Virginia. And all I want to do in response is watch incorruptible sunrises the rest of my life. It's an irresponsible reaction, but natural.

Evening -- The lake has returned to its seasonally typical condition, roaring in a strong north to northeast wind. The waves this afternoon and evening weren't quite so monumental as in past storms, but they still chewed on the beach and narrowed it to a strip of three or 4 feet of dry land.

Cool air from the north fed this wind. And it's clean air, so passing freighters stood in sharp relief against the pale sky. They were among the few vessels on Huron today. For a summer Saturday, the lake was remarkably underpopulated.

August 13, 2017

Fitz and I've been down to the lake three times today, a sensational day.

The sun has been generous and consistent, the wind barely a puff, the temperature mild. Because I am sick, each trip has lasted only about five minutes. I feel a little bit like a kid shut out of a birthday party. People are enjoying the lake in every possible way. Some are swimming, some are canoeing or kayaking, some are sailing, some are powerboating, some are riding *Huron Lady II*, the tourist boat. The best that I can do is take a photograph or two.

Photographs associate themselves with memories over time. And I find photographs about Great Lakes summers become more poignant with years. I'm thinking right now of the winter. There is no more bittersweet scene in January than a photograph of lake frolic from August. At the moment you view it, you will do anything to enjoy that moment now, or more realistically, to stay alive long enough to enjoy it when it happens again.

Lakes really are a mirror of our own spirits and selves. They are themselves also but we ascribe much to them. If they are stormy you may feel a storm inside. If they're tranquil they may move you to peace. The lake is bigger than any one of us, but it is also no bigger than our collective ability to destroy, rescue or project.

August 14, 2017

Today the lake was again at its finest. It was placid, not convulsive; it was light blue, not angry brown; it smiled under a fair sky, instead of scowling under a black cloud.

These things become the background unless you pay attention. One of the regrets I've had living in this place is that it is an office and not just a home. That it is an office is a professional advantage for me. Instead of spending hours commuting to get to my workplace I can walk a few feet and begin my work day.

On the other hand, I have just enough of a work ethic to feel I should be looking down at my laptop or on the phone to earn my pay. Which means that the lake, the air, the land all become scenery, not reality.

When I do look, I puzzle over basic physical facts. Why, when you are looking at the lake from a distance can you imagine it to be actually a wall?

Vertical, not horizontal. I only recently remarked on this phenomenon.

One of the signature experiences for any Michigander who does not live on the shoreline is to get out of the car, walk a short distance, come around the bend of the trail and suddenly behold the lake. That benevolent and boundless field of blue. There is nothing that defines summer better in the Great Lakes State. And I live with that every day when I come out of the bathroom in the morning and turn left.

August 15, 2017

I'm looking at the monthly bulletin of lake levels for the Great Lakes issued by the US Army Corps of Engineers Detroit district. It's for July 2017. It shows that all five Great Lakes plus Lake St. Clair are fairly close to their all-time highs. Lake Ontario, it appears, topped its all-time high in June and perhaps in May. All are expected to fall seasonally, but not necessarily by very much.

This all reminds me of the assertions by conspiracy theorists that the IJC or some other central agency is manipulating lake levels for unknown reasons. Unknown reasons, but with malicious intent or indifference to shoreline property owners. The old bromide comes to mind: government is too feckless coordinate anything, let alone a conspiracy.

We don't seem to be able to accept the fact that the lakes naturally cycle. The cycle is going to be disrupted by climate change, if it has not already been disrupted. A climatologist can make the case that the recent surge in lake levels is related to unusually heavy storms that may be associated with climate change.

My lake, represented by the Corps as Michigan-Huron, is less likely to top all time high records. Based on these charts it appears to be in the moderate upper range. Approximately 2 feet above the average but several feet below the record. It'll be interesting to see what happens to that level in the next couple of months.

August 18, 2017

With Fitz vacationing at a friend's house in anticipation of my departure for another trip to Traverse City, I stepped into the dark the other night to sit on the bench overlooking the small beach and large lake. It was around 1 am. A well illuminated vessel was heading north out of the river. Its engines were inaudible.

For some reason, I thought it might be a tourist cruise, like one Tom and I spotted last summer. But when I returned to the cottage I found it was the *Saginaw*, a 632-foot long freighter headed for Meldrum Bay, an Ontario port of which I'd never heard. It was doing 13.9 knots.

Something about the deep night, almost festive lights, the freighter's temporary anonymity and the stealthy waters gives a scene like this a dreamlike aspect. You aren't sure you're seeing what you think you're seeing.

August 19, 2017

Fitz and I arrived home about 10:30 pm but I have not gone down to the lake. My good intention as always is to greet it and the sunrise together.

A friend and I spent hours talking about groundwater before I left Traverse City. We're the State Capitol Groundwater Gurus of the 80s, when society was first becoming aware on a mass scale of groundwater because it was contaminated and people were scared. Now it is still contaminated and people have largely moved on.

I reminded him of a fact: the volume of groundwater in the Great Lakes is roughly equal to that of Lake Huron. So we have a sixth Great Lake.

I wanted to know how much groundwater contributes to my lake, Huron, and found that the figure is 72% as a component of streamflow. I give thanks for groundwater.

August 20, 2017

We missed the sunrise, but not by much. It was a starkly beautiful scene. An orange rim at the horizon, a cloudless, pale zenith. The sands of the narrow beach seemed cleansed, almost white. Not a living thing in sight, except the breathing, stirring lake.

Later – it was peak summer out on the sun-tinted lake this afternoon. Power boats grunted while smaller craft whined, some tugging water skiers. Swimmers in the placid waters had no need of life jackets. On a neighbor's beach, just the other side of the still-dammed creek, beer toting revelers in too-revealing swimwear mostly minded their manners. The calm lake contributed to the feeling of lazy summer.

Meanwhile, a few miles south where the lake drains into the St. Clair River, the annual Float Down caused authorities the annual headaches. It's an unsanctioned and to the government unwelcome custom where thousands of amateur sailors take to barely seaworthy inflatable rafts and inner tubes and clog the shipping lanes, leading authorities to halt freighter traffic. The local newspaper is reporting "2 arrests made, 3 lives saved." One of the lives belonged to a woman who was "treading water holding her purse above her head and having a hard time staying above the water," according to the police. Last year a howling wind drove 1500 floaters onto the Canadian shore, where they were detained and processed before being allowed to return to the homeland.

I realize the lake in some ways is a talisman. On good days when you are here it is a benevolent ever-present reassurance, fortifying you with strength even though you may not be conscious of it. On stormy winter days, it is the truth you don't want to admit, the unrelenting reminder of the ominous. Either way, it is beyond human control, in a universe that may well be indifferent to – or worse, unknowing of – our existence and fate.

August 21, 2017

It is becoming more difficult to type this journal again. Parkinson's is stiffening my fingers. If there is grace in this, it is that I am again grateful for the two years of relief I've been given. I might not have been able to observe and love Huron had I continued to deteriorate as I was in the spring of 2015. At that time, I shunned shirts with buttons because it took me 15 to 20 minutes to fasten them.

Today featured the solar eclipse. I don't feel misled as some radio voices said they were, but it was a disappointment. I had hoped the gloom would gather to the point where the lake would change colors, but the darkening of daylight was no more severe than what a summer haze could do.

The lake and sky did produce one interesting effect: a silver layer at the horizon that could trick an observer not paying close attention into believing freighters rode in air. This reminded me of the Great Lakes ghost ships I read about during adolescence. The most famous is the SS *Bannockburn*, which wrecked in November 1902 in Lake Superior while headed for Georgian Bay. Authorities recovered only a single life jacket. The mystery of the *Bannockburn's* sinking lay idle, waiting for the right person to resolve it. Instead, sailors and captains began to spot a ship of the size and shape of the *Bannockburn* sailing past.

"These sightings happen during or just before storms, fog, and other bad weather and seem to be warnings of danger. Most of these sightings come in the month of November as well," says blogger Joe C. Combs. The Great Lakes are large enough to produce legends.

August 22, 2017

It was a good sunrise. The sun plays such delightful tricks with the water, turning it silver, orange, gold or deep blue. Today the sun turned the gray lake to buttery yellow when it pressed its nose against a temporary window in the clouds.

It occurred to me today how few forms of life I've seen on the beach beyond the king and queen of them all, *homo sapiens*. A dead gull, a dead fish, zebra mussel shells; live gulls aplenty, a fish or two in the shallows, songbirds set back from the water. There is much more biological diversity than that, but it is not evident from the narrow perspective I hold.

In a sense, all but a few of us are in that position, deep inside a realm of breathtaking and staggeringly complex life forms, but barely aware of it. The true measure of character is how curious one is to learn, and I don't score high on that scale.

August 23, 2017

Tom is here and I again see the lake through his eyes. On a cool day that occasionally yielded sprinkles, he spent an hour and a half in Huron. He treasures what I sometimes take for granted.

It turns my thoughts to the visionaries who pioneered state and regional parks and park policies around here beginning a century ago. One of their goals was to make available to people of modest or less means opportunities to enjoy the outdoors – for everything from picnicking to swimming. The working class was in the minds of these planners. I think of the early assembly line workers who labored under conditions that could drain any one of joy and who could never afford to buy lakefront land. With parks, they could imagine themselves wealthy. For next to nothing in admission they could have access to endless waters and so could their families.

We must hold fast to these policies.

August 24, 2017

It's early afternoon and the *Harbour Fountain* and *Golden Oak* are both anchored in Sarnia's aquatic parking lot, directly offshore of this point by a few miles. Tom and I walked Fitz along the river in town this morning and saw the *Harbour Fountain* head up and out into the lake. We also saw a diving marker, pleasure craft and the *Algoma Equinox*, downbound. These huge tankers sliding up and down such a narrow passage remind me of wingless jumbo jets heading through Manhattan.

Later – Tom and I chose to dine at a new restaurant on the river south of town. The online menu was enticing, but when we arrived the hostess said the grill was down due to a missing part and 2/3 of the menu was also down. We stayed. Accordingly, the chief joy of the meal was watching two freighters pass going in opposite directions.

Cold and wind have disturbed the lake the last two days. All day and night the lake has breathed thickly, like a smoker.

August 25, 2017

Tom spent a half hour alone by the lake before leaving around noon. I, not he, characterize it as a reverential experience. He seems to draw sustenance from the lake merely by standing or sitting beside it.

On a related note, I proposed to Tom that there ought to be a zone of reverence 1000 feet back from the shore. It seems disrespectful that in traversing the first few hundred feet away from the lake you go from the relative wild to the sputtering of trucks and the annoyed whine of car whose drivers are unable to pass them. You go from authentic water to the artifice of flashing billboards and gaudy storefronts. It's profane.

When I walked Fitz down to the shore this afternoon a plume of black smoke rose from the distant Ontario show. This is what distance, as afforded by the openness of the lake surface, does to me: it inspires my deepest curiosity and even awe. I wanted to know what was happening at the base of the column of black smoke, where far was near.

The waves of the last few days, ushered along by the persistent, even nagging north to northeast winds, have rearranged the stones on the beach again.

The *Harbour Fountain* just exited the parking lot and is moving toward Sarnia at 8 knots, but the *Algoma Hansa* glitters while stationary offshore of this place.

August 26, 2017

This is how it happens. How age outruns you and death files its claim for you. Another summer has almost passed with hardly a moment's pause. The only memories that I will carry for any length of time are the sunrises, especially the typical quiet, the world's expectant hush, just before the appearance of the sun on the lake rim.

A sign of fall on the Great Lakes is a waterspout, and I saw one forming the other day. Cool air over warm water creates friction which turns into spin. Our waterspouts are more monumental than temperamental. They're like a giant's long legs that come down from the clouds, dance on the lake and withdraw from the dance floor. This one was ephemeral, being born and dying within a few minutes, a life span above water even more brief than a mayfly's.

Speaking of which, I puzzle over the purpose of life when I think of the Great Lakes mayfly. Members of the order *Ephemeroptera*, mayflies can spend mere hours to a day or two in flight as adults after years burrowed in lake sediments. They reproduce and die. This is a form of life in which the individual is meaningless. Only the mass matters.

And the mass of adults is so mammoth that after they molt and take to the air, their flight is captured on Weather Service radar. They pile up under lights and at least one coastal town in Ohio turned a snow plow loose on their corpses.

They're very sensitive to pollutants. Their resurgence telegraphs the good news that the lake is recovering. It also reminds me that the natural world proceeds unperturbed while we try in futility to discern its meaning.

August 27, 2017

I tried to find a Petoskey stone on the beach today. I failed. That's the typical result. To me, they are impossible to spot unless they're wet, and even then my chances are slim. But why do I even look? It's a Michigan thing.

The Petoskey stone's origins distinguish it from other rocks. Its distinct (when wet) honeycomb mottling reveals corals from seas that covered Michigan 350 million years ago. When the corals died sediment covered them and they became part of the Alpena Limestone. So, like limestone generally, the Petoskey stone is drab. So rock lovers polish them.

There is evidence that Michiganders are more likely to appreciate Petoskey stones. In the *New York Times* this spring, Eric Spitznagel wrote: "My first gift to my future wife [who was not from Michigan], a month after we'd started dating, was a Petoskey necklace. She looked at it as if I'd just handed her a macaroni bracelet. 'Are you being serious?' she asked."

When I moved here, I gave no thought to Petoskey stones. I assumed they were well north. An MSU on-line textbook says, "The Petoskey stone can be found anywhere in the state from the Traverse City area across the state to Alpena." That excludes this area by over 150 miles. But collectors showed me otherwise within weeks.

August 28, 2017

Around 10 p.m. Saturday, I took Fitz out to empty his bladder. Turning around when he was done, I was startled to see, through the gap between two cottages, a glittering vessel heading south. It was just a freighter but it reminded me of a pirate ship with torches ablaze.

My friend down on Lake Erie's shore sent me an appalling eight-second video yesterday. It featured pulsing green water with what appeared to be a stain of gray-white mixing in. Algae and perhaps microcystin, killer of dogs and attacker of people. Erie is critically ill again and all the work of well-meaning people won't save it without the force of law. Unfortunately, we need laws and enforcement to prevent farmers from spreading manure and fertilizer where it will run immediately off into water. Unfortunately, we need and don't have lawmakers with the guts to enact to pass such laws.

There is nothing like that repugnant algae on my stretch of Huron. The major sources of phosphorus are far away, the current swift, the water deep, all unlike Erie. But if I drove 50 miles north of home and rounded the tip of the Thumb, I would come across the ugliness of algae-ridden Saginaw Bay.

Around midnight last night came the bellowing of two ship horns. It wasn't the proverbial mourning sound, more like an aural equivalent of male marking. In a light fog I could see only lights, but the Boatnerd web site revealed that the *Honorable James L. Oberstar*, heading north, was passing the southbound *John G. Munson*. Oberstar of Minnesota: longtime chair of the U.S. House of Representatives infrastructure committee, which also had power over the Clean Water Act and navigation. He is remembered fondly by several constituencies. There is life after death: the vessel bearing his name passes by regularly.

August 29, 2017

I'm staying with my friends in Leelanau again. Their hospitality is unflagging. Tonight, a lovely pink sunset over Lake Michigan was visible but I remembered sunrises back over beloved Huron. In two years my allegiance has shifted from MI to H. It has been good to me, an ever-present companion.

August 30, 2017

Recently I tweeted a photo of Grand Traverse Bay under a colorful post-sunset sky with the words, "Politicians may fail us but nature never will." Although that captured my sentiment at the moment of tweeting, I knew then and now that reality is more complicated. What does it mean for nature to fail us? Nature is indifferent to us.

Nature's indifference has been demonstrated in Texas the past few days. The epic floods have killed two dozen people and displaced thousands. Although perhaps promoted by climate change, this event was a part of the cycle – nature's alternating wrath and kindness.

SEPTEMBER

The door slammed shut on summer today, and the lake both foreshadowed and reflected it.

September 1, 2017

I arrived back at the lake at about 3:30 this morning. I could hear the lake thrashing in a strong breeze but did not go down to look at it until after sunrise. As has often been true this summer, the wind is from the east and is driving water against the shore. The creek is still unable to reach the lake because of a large sandbar created by the waves.

The beach, such as it is, has a new necklace of pebbles arranged differently from the last storm. A small tree from the neighbor's yard has tumbled into the sand after its roots were exposed by wave action. Fitz found the scent of something in the pebbles. He would not readily retreat from the beach when I called for him. Glistening in the sun, some objects appeared to be beach glass, but when I moved I saw that they were just wet rock.

Autumn is an interloper this year. According to tradition, three weeks of summer remain, but along the way last night the temperature dipped as low as 43 and it is only about 60 here. Accompanying the cooler air is a lower sun. Waves now have deeper shadows, which create a stippling effect on the surface of the water. Tom plans to visit tomorrow for a final summer swim, but I worry that he may find the water unwelcoming.

Given the cold and the fierce wind, few craft traversed the surface of Huron this afternoon. I counted two sailboats, three powerboats and two freighters in the panorama out back. On land, things were busier. Lakeshore Drive out front ran thick with vehicles heading north.

Like a dog eating grass, my body remembers what I cannot put into words. In this case it is preparation for winter. Already, I think of the necessity as well as the pleasure of wearing thicker outerwear and sipping hot beverages on cold mornings. I also remember how this lake looks in winter. It is a frigid beauty unconcerned with human aesthetic criteria on the worst days.

September 2, 2017

This morning's sunrise – or at least immediate post sunrise since I didn't get up in time – reminded me of a desert sunrise. The sky was a sandy tan color. The sun was an orange almost feverish orb. Water made the difference. The easterly breeze persisted and the water tossed green and blue, depending on where the sun struck.

65

I took a photo or two, of course, and both tweeted one and posted one on Facebook. At least on Facebook, I've developed quite a reputation amongst my friends for my sunrise shots. I think I've been a good promoter of tourism for the eastern shore of Michigan. I hear remarks about it when I run into a Facebook friend.

Although the wind has subsided, the lake continues to hurl itself against the beach. But now it's making a little progress in consuming the sand.

It's mid-afternoon and I'm awaiting the arrival of Tom. I worry because the abundant sunshine and relative warmth of the day so far threatens to turn into a cloudy drizzle. I'd hate it if he couldn't enjoy at least an hour on the beach in the water.

Later – After dinner we parked beside the river and in the darkness and drizzle watched two northbound freighters churn the water. The *Edgar B. Speer* is headed to Duluth and the *Herbert C Jackson* to Saginaw.

September 3, 2017

After a heavy early morning rain, the skies cleared this afternoon and the lake opened up like the promise of summer, now ending. Fitz and I stood on Debbie's patio as others loitered on the beach and on the bench above the sand. A smattering of jet skis, powerboats and other craft dotted the lake surface under an increasingly benevolent sun.

After dinner, my pal Fitz and I returned to the beach, now abandoned, as was the lake, by and large. A waxing moon hung from a contrail in a pink orange sky. White swells loped toward the shore. I love evenings by the lake. They make order of a cluttered day; the cleanse and they reassure.

September 4, 2017

The door slammed shut on summer today, and the lake both foreshadowed and reflected it.

Early this morning, not long after sunrise, the lake was uneasy. Restless. Something was going to happen today. The yellow sky and the bloodshot sun said as much.

As the day warmed, one could've imagined it was July. I was startled to look out the window and see waves moving south to north. That has rarely happened this summer.

At about 4 o'clock, I drove into town to meet two friends returning from Port Austin. Our meal began under the same yellow sky, but after an hour and a half the yellow yielded to black.

I rushed back to the cottage to take care of Fitz. He was fine, but when I looked out the window in the gray gloom of mid evening, the lake had turned around. Waves were running north to south. Sheets of rain reached down like bristles on a paintbrush here and there on the lake surface.

Back on land, the many cars that had occupied this community's parking spaces were gone. The people who had been swimming, boating, and sailing just three or four hours previously were gone. Summer was gone.

The lake was still there. Gray, green, still uneasy, but unconcerned what season it was.

September 6, 2017

In childhood, I had several obsessions. One was highways. I loved miniature highway sets. With Jack and especially Tom, I built small freeway networks on the train table in the basement. I imagined myself traveling to distant lands on the roads those toys represented.

So now, as I look at the signs on the lake roads, the past comes rushing back. As someone who grew up thinking roads to be supreme, it startles me to see a sign saying that the road abruptly ends under command of the lake. But of course it does. No road continues into a lake.

Two different signs warn motorists not to proceed. One says, no outlet. The other says, in classic language, dead end. It seems so harsh. Arriving at the terminus of the road does not mean it or you are dead.

So "no outlet" is preferable to me. No outlet reminds me of the great basin of the west, from which the water cannot escape. Here we have just the opposite. The water at the end of the road drains almost eagerly into the ocean.

One of my childish conceits was the idea of building a bridge across one of the Great Lakes. Since I didn't think much of Lake Huron in those days, the span I imagined linked Muskegon to Milwaukee.

Roads stirred my imagination and childhood even more than the panorama of water that I saw from the back of the station wagon as we headed north to visit grandma and grandpa. Now, late in life, it's roads that I fear and water I welcome.

September 8, 2017

During a meeting today with a friend, I learned that a major public figure in Michigan has a soft spot for Lake Huron. I sat up straight.

She didn't know why he has regard for Lake Huron but she speculated, probably accurately, the gentleman owns property on the lake. That's where most of us get our love of a place; we live there.

If I could sit down with him to talk about Lake Huron, we would have a lot to discuss.

I would talk about the sunrises here, what they have meant to me as I've tried to rebuild, or make sense of my life.

I would talk about the lonely shores of the northeast corner of Michigan where the dwarf lake iris predominates. Like those shores it is exquisite and little known.

I would talk about the view from the east, in Canada. How it reminds me so much of the view from Michigan's west shore over Lake Michigan, but with fewer spectators. And how the low dunes of the Ontario shore mimic those of west Michigan.

I would ask him whether we want the forgotten lake to remain forgotten perhaps. There are five Great Lakes, and perhaps one of them can remain anonymous. Does everything have to be known, plotted, and exploited? Maybe Huron is the lake that reminds us when it's time to stop.

September 9, 2017

Sometimes you know you are near a lake without seeing it. One such case is at the roadside. Today I passed a pontoon boat with a price and a phone number on the sign attached to it, and another sign that said hoist for sale. When I saw the latter, I immediately wondered if the owner was giving up on watching about during these high-water times.

Today's wind is not fierce as it has been on previous weekends. Light to moderate, would be my description. But the water is so high that even a moderate motion produces a splash that rockets far above the sea wall. As Fitz sniffed in the pile of rocks on the side of the wall, a stream of water rose from the south side inches from his face and startled him backwards.

September 10, 2017

This morning, Fitz and I took breakfast on the patio. It's not my patio. It belongs to my landlord who is a good friend. She gladly shares it with friends and neighbors – and a tenant.

It was one of those hazy fall mornings. The lake had calmed down since yesterday and the breeze did not temper the warm sun much. I feel privileged to be within 100 feet of a great lake on a lovely morning.

The lake and its people proceeded in their single-minded way. A stream of freighters ran both north and south. A trio of powerboats shot down the lake towards Port Huron. A couple of kayakers paddled almost to the place where I was sitting but then turned around. The lake stayed as it was, with audible but not overwhelming waves breaking on the beach.

There was an ache, too. I always have an ache on Sundays, reaching back to childhood, when I dreaded the return to school. But this ache is deeper. It comes from the possibility that I'll separate myself from this place for economic reasons.

I never expected Lake Huron's shores to become home but they have. If this is one of the last Sundays I get to treasure the lake from the patio, at least all this morning's moments will leave in their wake a peace and contentment it is difficult to find in life.

LAKE HURON

Lake Huron is named for the Wyandot Indians, or Hurons, who lived there.

Lake Huron is the second largest Great Lake by surface area and the fifth largest freshwater lake in the world.

It has the longest shoreline of the Great Lakes, counting the shorelines of its 30,000 islands.

Manitoulin Island is the largest freshwater island in the world.

Georgian Bay and Saginaw Bay are the two largest bays on the Great Lakes.

Early explorers listed Georgian Bay as a separate sixth lake because it is nearly separated from the rest of Lake Huron by Manitoulin Island and the Bruce Peninsula.

Georgian Bay is large enough to be among the world's 20 largest lakes.

On Nov. 9, 1913, the worst storm ever to hit the Great Lakes struck Lake Huron. Wind gusts of 90 mph and waves of more than 35 feet sank 10 ships and killed 235 seamen.
.

LENGTH: 206 miles

BREADTH: 183 miles

AVERAGE DEPTH: 195 ft.

MAXIMUM DEPTH: 750 ft. / 229 m.

WATER SURFACE AREA: 23,000 sq. miles

SHORELINE LENGTH (including islands): 3,827 miles

RETENTION/REPLACEMENT TIME: 22 years

Sources: Great Lakes Commission

U.S. EPA, The Great Lakes: An Environmental Atlas and Resource Book

A lurid flush of sunset sky,
An angry sketch of gleaming lake,
I will remember till I die
The sound, of pines that sob and sigh,
Of waves upon the beach that break.

August Evening on the Beach, Lake Huron
William Wilfrid Campbell

FLOW (For Love of Water)

FLOW is dedicated to protecting and preserving the extraordinary and essential natural resource endowment known as the Great Lakes by applying public trust principles to educate, advance policy, and provide solutions to the pressing water issues facing the region, nation and planet.

Containing 20% of the world's available surface freshwater, the Great Lakes are often referred to as North America's "crown jewels." They are, without question, precious and valuable – but they are much more. The Great Lakes are globally unique; they are a magnificent natural resource endowment existing nowhere else on the earth.

By ancient law, passed on from Roman times to the Magna Carta to the Northwest Ordinance, the Great Lakes are a "public trust" – waters and bottomlands held in trust for the benefit of public to use and enjoy. With that trust comes a duty of stewardship, what the courts have called a "perpetual and solemn duty" to protect the Great Lakes for our use and enjoyment, our children's, and that of future generations.

By employing best science and law, FLOW empowers citizens and communities with public trust strategies to protect the water of the Great Lakes Basin for current and future generations.

About Dave Dempsey

Dave Dempsey has authored four books and co-authored four more on conservation, the Great Lakes, and Michigan writers. He has been active in Michigan conservation and environmental policy since 1981.

Fitz

Made in the USA
Monee, IL
09 September 2023

42336603R00044